SCANDIKITCHEN
THE ESSENCE OF
HYGGE

SCANDIKITCHEN
THE ESSENCE OF
HYGGE

BRONTË AURELL

RYLAND PETERS & SMALL
LONDON • NEW YORK

Designer Emily Breen
Editor Miriam Catley
Production Mai-Ling Collyer
Art director Leslie Harrington
Editorial director Julia Charles
Publisher Cindy Richards

With photography by Peter Cassidy

First published in 2017 by Ryland Peters & Small
20–21 Jockey's Fields, London WC1R 4BW
and 341 E 116th St, New York NY 10029

www.rylandpeters.com

10 9 8 7 6 5 4 3 2

Printed in Slovenia

A CIP record for this book is available from
the British Library.

US Library of Congress Cataloging-in-Publication
Data has been applied for.

CONTENTS

Introduction **6**

INTRODUCTION

A little over a year ago, the word 'hygge' first entered the English language. Obscure and unpronounceable, it was initially ignored and left in the corner, while people wondered what on earth it was, what to do with it and why anyone bothered taking it out of Scandinavia in the first place.

Then something happened. Mindfulness needed a buddy, the media needed the next big thing and hygge was just there, being relaxed and quite at peace with itself, not bothering anyone, not trying to impress anyone – just simply enjoying... being.

The hygge-whirlwind that has followed has been so uncharacteristic of good old trusty hygge, that it has ended up almost a shadow of its former self at times. Thrust onto a brightly-lit stage, into the glaring limelight, hygge has been the star, been hailed as a saviour of all things mankind – and even had blankets, sweaters and candles named after it.

Along the way, poor hygge lost some of the essence of what it really means. Hygge was hyped to such heights that new media eventually had to drop it – and now the hygge backlash has begun. As a friend put it: 'Hygge is a lot less hyggelig now it's for sale'.

The thing with hygge is that it isn't complicated. It is all about being present in the moment. You know how to hygge already and you don't really need anyone to teach you the basics. You most certainly do not need to buy any 'stuff' to be feeling more hyggelig in your life.

On the other hand, perhaps there is a reason you picked up this book in the first place. Hygge in its purest form is definitely something we are all longing to bring back into our day-to-day lives; to find a way to be present a bit more. Having a word for this in the English language means that we now have more power to consciously make it happen as and when we want to.

This book is a little pocket book about hygge. It is about what hygge is – and also what it isn't. The book is filled with a collection of yummy

treats to bake at home – treats to enjoy together with people you enjoy spending time with, because hygge in its purest form is simply about togetherness and appreciating life. Treats and hygge go together – and adding a home-baked cake to the table is a sure-fire way to slow things down, enjoy and just... be.

Harmony
Wellbeing
Content
Moments
Stressfree
Candles
Peaceful
Warmth
Calm
Relax
Comfort
Present
Happy
Cosiness
Safe
Complete
Quality-time
Togetherness
Emotions
Log-fire
Sharing
Snug
Family
Relaxing
Wholesome

chapter 1

HYGGE AND... THE BASICS

*Don't hurry, don't worry,
you're only here for a short
visit, so be sure to smell the
flowers along the way.*

WALTER HAGEN

THE WORD 'HYGGE'

The word 'hygge' can be traced back to Old Norse, when the Vikings used the verb hyggja, which meant 'to think and to be satisfied with'. The word also has roots in Old English in the word hycgan, which meant 'to think and to consider'.

Hygge has been used in Norwegian and Danish for the past few hundred years, and it is widely understood across all of the Nordic countries. While the word is used in Norwegian today, it is used more frequently in the Danish language. A Dane will use the word several times every single day – as a verb used to describe seasons and feelings, something ironic or even scary.

The word 'hug' also has connections to the word hygge. Imagine the feeling of hugging someone. You can't genuinely hug someone without giving a bit of yourself and letting go, even if it is just for a moment. That feeling, the split second when two people both relax into a hug, is similar to the feeling of hygge – except hygge isn't over in a few seconds, but simply lasts as long as it lasts, with no defined time attached to it.

People often confuse the word hygge with the word cosy. Cosiness, however, is mostly defined and created by physical things around you, whereas hygge is a completely psychological and emotional state.

HOW TO PRONOUNCE HYGGE
'who-guh'

How you prononounce hygge does depend where you are from, what language you usually speak and how you pronounce the 'hy' sound and the 'gge' sound in your own language. This is a good steer for a British English speaker, less so for a French speaker.

There is a slight variation between the Norwegian and Danish pronunciation of hygge. Few will even pick up on the variation, though, and if you use 'who-guh', you'll be closer than most pronunciation guides of late. One thing is for sure, though – it never, ever rhymes with jiggy!

HOW TO USE THE WORD HYGGE

It is natural that when a word is adopted into another language, the use of the word will change over time. Does it matter how you use the word? Not really – a language evolves when the words grow and migrate into uses in other cultures. However the word is used outside of the Nordic shores, the correct ways to use it are as follows:

Hygge is a verb
To hygge, with r-added for when you are doing it.
For example:
We are going to hygge later.
We hygger now.

Hygge is often used together with common nouns
When hygge is used with a common noun it becomes hyggelig (or hyggeligt, as we have gender specific words).

For example:
The cottage is really hyggelig.
We had a hyggelig time at the party.
Your house feels very hyggeligt.
It was so hyggeligt you could visit us today.

Plural
The form is always hyggelige.

Incorrect use of hygge
(if you are using a Scandinavian language base):

I'm going to have hygge now. (Correct use: I'm going to hygge now.)
Let's go find some hygge. (Correct use: Let's go and hygge.)
The room is hygge. (Correct use: The room is hyggeligt.)
I don't like this café, it is just not hygge.
(Correct use: I don't like this café, it is not hyggelig.)
The party was hygge. (Correct use: The party was hyggelig.)

OTHER WAYS TO USE THE WORD HYGGE

In Denmark, hygge is such a huge part of the culture and what defines the Danish people and psyche that it is referred to many times daily. Everything is related back to this state of mind.

Uhygge Literally: Un-hygge. It means scary or sinister. Horror movies are uhyggelige.

Råhygge Hygge slang, literally: raw hygge. This is when hygge is so good, so pure, that it is bigger than hygge. For example: You've planned a family night in, everybody is having a great time and then someone adds more snacks. Someone might then say: 'Oh, this is raw hygge!'

Adding hygge to an event Every season can have hygge added in front to give it instant hygge appeal. For example, Julehygge is Christmas hygge (every event during the festive season). Sommerhygge is Summer hygge – the kind you have when you are on your summer holidays. Påskehygge is Easter hygge and so on. Familiehygge – family hygge – is often used to plan weekend time with loved ones.

Suggestive hygge throughout the day 'Shall we meet up after work to hygge? I'll get some snacks, will you chill the wine?'

Adding hygge to the days of the week Fredagshygge (Friday hygge) is often used to describe planned evenings in on Friday nights. Monday hygge is less common!

Reinforcing hygge If you've been to see someone and you meet them again, you often say 'That was hyggeligt last time' – to reinforce that you had a lovely time and ensuring others felt the same.

As an encouragement Ha' det hyggeligt means 'Have hygge' – you can say this to people who are going off somewhere as a parting sentence.

Sarcastic hygge The word is sometimes used sarcastically, to denote something uhyggeligt. For example: Running a marathon? How hyggeligt!

Hyggesnakke To hygge-talk. This refers to having a chat with someone solely for the purpose of just chatting.

Hyggestemning Hygge ambiance. Stemning is a word often used to describe an atmospheric ambiance or mood. If there is a good stemning in the air, hygge can develop. In order to find hygge, the stemning – the ambiance or mood – has to be there first. It sets the scene for hygge and it is suggestive of what might happen later on.

chapter 2

HYGGE AND... HAPPINESS

Happiness is when what you think, what you say, and what you do are in harmony.

MAHATMA GANDHI

The happiest nations in the world

The list of the happiest nations in the world is usually topped by all the Scandinavian countries (actually, usually topped by us Danes who are never shy of using this best-at-being-happy fact to sell trips to see the Little Mermaid). These lists are calculated from a series of important factors ranging from society to economy and culture. Sure, they do ask the question 'Are you happy?', but the weighting is all based on statistics rather than our own personal interpretation of what happy is. This is with good reason: happy is really hard to define.

You can't really define what happiness means without using a synonym for the word and everything you then base it on becomes so subjective. How do you know when you are happy? Well, when you are happy!

Nobody has asked every person across the Nordics if they really feel happy. The answers would be far too subjective and you'd never be able to fit it into a chart or make it a statistic. The answer to the Scandinavian apparent abundance of happiness lies much more in our general belief in life and society – and in our place in the world.

I'm often asked about why Danes (and Scandinavians in general) are so happy. I usually omit mentioning that Scandinavians are among the highest users of anti-depressants in the EU – mainly because a general sense of happiness doesn't (and shouldn't) always come down to this.

People are prescribed anti-depressants for many reasons. Even in depression, there can be pockets of happiness (and there also has to be, if people are to feel they can eventually recover).

In recent times, hygge has been hailed as one of the factors to the Scandinavian abundance of happiness. To understand the basic happiness in Scandinavia, it is worthwhile taking a look at the social care system. It is set up to ensure that every person is looked after and protected to a certain level and allowed to live inside this clearly defined structure. In short, our needs are met by and large. We don't really have anything to complain about.

Hygge fits in when you start to appreciate the way Scandinavian countries work. We have time to be with our families because we don't work too many hours and we all get to take several weeks of vacation every year and our kids will never have to pay to go to university.

I don't think it is wrong to assume that feeling safe plays a big part in our happiness in general – and that this also leads to hyggelige times with friends and family where we consciously allow ourselves to fleetingly appreciate that moment, as it happens: 'Yes, we are having a lovely time and I appreciate the hyggelige time I am having – how nice this is'.

Hygge comes with the allocation of space and time to relax and allow yourself to be happy and appreciating your sense of self and the people around you. In a sense, in order to bring more hygge to your life, you

The purpose of memory

Scientifically, it's important to remember the purpose of memory when it comes to happiness. The hippocampus in the brain is responsible for happy memories – and the serotonin (a neurotransmitter) in the brain then helps regulate mood, sleep, appetite etc. These two in combination have a huge effect on how happy we may perceive ourselves to be. For example, a brisk walk for 20 minutes on a nice day boosts your mood, helps you to think clearer and also helps keep your brain and memory active. Exercise – in all forms – helps release endorphins and proteins that make the brain happier, and thus, you too.

need to make room for it – and by making room to do absolutely nothing apart from having a nice time with people you like, you will inevitably start to relax, at least at some point. If you don't have to worry too much about all the things that go on outside your front door, this might well come easier to you. It is about protecting your own pocket of life.

If you leave work at 5pm on the dot, walk home instead of taking the train, take a short cut through the park, notice the birds singing... the time you gain is you reclaiming your life. Take it back. You do not owe anything to anyone else once you leave your desk.

Will it make you happy to leave work earlier and consciously create time to hygge with your friends and family? It may not make your boss happy, granted, but yes, it will most certainly make you happier in the long term. Is it easy to start leaving work at 5pm when you usually leave at 8pm? Nope, absolutely not, but it is about choices. You cannot possibly fit everything into the 24 hours you have been allocated – so you need to decide which bits will make you feel better (and, yes, happier) – and then focus on those.

Scandinavians don't have to worry about leaving at 5pm, because it is considered a bad thing to stay late. There is no shame in leaving work on time in Scandinavia. Therein lies the biggest difference between the Scandinavian work culture and many big city work cultures around the world. While you can't change the way other people work, you can try to claw back a little time here and there to begin with – and hopefully, at some point, you will be able to create a little extra window of time in your day where you don't have to do anything at all. In this moment, hygge can often be found.

CARROT CAKE

Gulerodskage

150 g/³/₄ cup caster/granulated sugar

150 g/³/₄ cup light brown sugar

3 eggs

300 ml/1¹/₄ cups sunflower oil

300 g/2¹/₃ cups self-raising/rising flour or 2 cups cake flour mixed with 4 teaspoons baking powder

¹/₂ teaspoon salt

1 teaspoon vanilla sugar

2 teaspoons ground cinnamon

1 teaspoon mixed spice/apple pie spice

300 g/3 cups grated carrots

70 g/¹/₂ cup pine nuts

It's rare that I don't tire of a cake (trust me, I do eat a lot of cake). However, this carrot cake recipe is one that I started making over 12 years ago when I worked at innocent Drinks and we used to bring in cake every Friday for afternoon coffee breaks. It is still one of the most asked for recipes at ScandiKitchen and the first cake to sell out. Over time, the recipe has changed very little. What started out as a bet with Jonas about 'making the best carrot cake, like, ever' is still our favourite cake.

Preheat the oven to 160°C (325°F) Gas 3.

In a bowl, whisk the caster/granulated and light brown sugars together with the eggs until light and airy, gradually adding the oil.

In a separate bowl, sift the dry ingredients together, then fold into the sugar and egg mixture. Fold in the grated carrots, reserving a little for decorating the finished cake, then the pine nuts.

Pour the mixture into the prepared cake pans and bake in the preheated oven for about 25 minutes, or until a skewer inserted into the middle comes out clean. Turn out of the pans and leave to cool completely on a wire rack.

continued over page

continued from previous page

TOPPING:

300 g/1¹/₂ cups cream cheese

100 g/³/₄ cup icing/ confectioners' sugar, sifted

50 g/3¹/₂ tablespoons softened butter

freshly squeezed juice of 1 large lime

grated lime zest, to decorate

2 x 20-cm/8-in. round cake pans, greased and lined with baking parchment

SERVES 8

To make the topping, beat all the ingredients together well (4–5 minutes in a food mixer).

Arrange the first cake layer on a serving plate and spread over almost half of the topping evenly. Place the second cake bottom-up (so you get a perfectly flat top on your cake) on top and spread the rest of the topping over the cake. Decorate with the reserved grated carrots and lime zest.

AUNTIE INGA'S 'KLADDKAKA' STICKY CHOCOLATE CAKE

Kladdkaka

2 eggs

200 g/1 cup caster/
granulated sugar

150 g/1 cup plain/
all-purpose flour or
cake flour

3 tablespoons good-quality
cocoa powder (I use Fazer),
plus extra for dusting

1 tablespoon vanilla sugar
or extract

a pinch of salt

100 g/1 stick unsalted butter,
melted and cooled slightly

whipped cream, to serve

*a 20-cm/8-in. deep round
cake pan, greased and lined
with baking parchment*

SERVES 6-8

This cake is one of the most famous fika cakes in Sweden. Every café has a version of Kladdkaka (which literally means 'Sticky Cake'). It is a bit like an under-baked chocolate cake and that is exactly what makes it so very good. This is our Auntie Inga's recipe. It's an easy cake to make, but watch the baking: too little and it's a runny mess; too much and it's a stodgy, dry cake.

Preheat the oven to 180°C (350°F) Gas 4.

Whisk the eggs and sugar together until the mixture is light, fluffy and pale.

Sift all the dry ingredients into the egg and sugar mixture. Fold in until everything is incorporated, then fold in the melted butter.

Pour into the prepared cake pan.

Bake in the preheated oven for around 10–15 minutes. The exact time can vary, so keep an eye on the cake. A perfect kladdkaka is very, very soft in the middle, but not runny once it has cooled – but almost runny. The cake will not rise, but it will puff up slightly during baking.

If you press down gently on the cake, the crust should need a bit of pressure to crack. When this happens, the cake is done. Leave to cool in the pan.

Serve with whipped cream, dusted with cocoa powder.

RYE AND BLUEBERRY FLAPJACK

Råg och blåbärmueslibar

175 g/1 1/2 sticks butter

2 tablespoons golden/light corn syrup

1 tablespoon maple syrup

50 g/1/4 cup dark brown soft sugar

100 g/1/2 cup light brown soft sugar

1/2 teaspoon ground cinnamon

1/2 teaspoon vanilla sugar OR extract OR use the seeds from 1 vanilla pod/bean

100 g/1 cup jumbo oats

200 g/2 cups rye flakes

100 g/3/4 cup dried blueberries

a 20 x 30-cm/8 x 11 3/4-in. rectangular baking pan, greased and lined with baking parchment

MAKES 12

Who doesn't love a gooey, oaty flapjack bar? This one has the nice little twist of rye flakes added to the mixture. The consistency is a little different from your normal flapjack – the rye gives a more wholesome feel to the end result. Rye also has a deep almost nutty flavour to it, which I love. Add whatever dried berries or nuts tickle your fancy if you want to vary it a bit.

Preheat the oven to 160°C (325°F) Gas 3.

Put the butter, golden/light corn syrup, maple syrup and dark and light brown sugars into a saucepan. Heat together gently until just melted. Mix in the ground cinnamon and vanilla. Add the jumbo oats and rye flakes and stir well. Add the blueberries and stir again to evenly combine.

Spoon the mixture into the prepared pan. Pack the mixture down quite firmly using the back of a wooden spoon and press into all the corners (this will ensure you get a flapjack bar, not crumbs).

Bake in the preheated oven for around 20 minutes or until golden. The longer you bake, the crispier the result, so if you like your flapjack extra-chewy, take it out a little earlier.

Mark where the slices will be on the hot flapjack using a knife, then leave to cool completely in the pan before turning out and cutting properly into slices.

The flapjacks will keep well for at least a week stored in an airtight container.

chapter 3

HYGGE AND... SHARING

We should look for someone
to eat and drink with before
looking for something
to eat and drink.

EPICURUS

Fundamentally, humans like sharing.

Since time began, we have hunted and gathered and shared food with our families. In fact, this is also how many animals eat and this act of sharing has always been central to how we live.

Something magical happens when you bring food to a group of people. It quickly becomes the thing that connects you and instantly helps create a moment in which you gel together and find common purpose and common ground. Imagine your kitchen table – then place your three best friends there with you. Then add a basket of freshly baked buns, a bottle of wine or a delicious home-baked cake. In that exact moment you have created a circle of something warm, delicious and memorable. The moment has become elevated from a chat around a table to a shared experience of something that makes you all feel good. The conversation flows as you all share the experience of the flavours, textures and tastes.

Your brains ping subconscious messages when you eat, secretly awaking memories from childhood and other events in our life. Sweet treats especially will help release happy feelings in your brain, which is why we often crave these and find it hard to stop reaching for them.

I once discussed this deep-rooted desire and love of sharing food with a friend. She said she had thought for ages that her children absolutely loved roast chicken. They loved it so much, that they started asking for roast chicken all the time, not just for Sunday lunch. She couldn't quite understand why and then, one day, the penny dropped: the kids didn't care about the chicken, but it was the only time the family actually sat down and ate together in the week. Sunday afternoon roast chicken had become that special moment when they connected, switched off from the rest of the world and tuned into each other as a family. The hyggelige Sundays with no phones, nobody else than just family present, were regarded by the children as the best thing of their whole week, even if they didn't realise why or couldn't explain it. Soon, the family started having dinners together most evenings. And, while the kids still loved roast chicken, everybody understood that the thing they were missing the most was each other, even if they had spent every evening in the same room.

Back in the days of my old life when I worked for a lovely smoothie company in London, we wanted to make sure that people reconnected with each other in the office. The company had grown quickly and people had started eating at their desk, forgetting to take breaks and it had started to feel a bit stressful. We decided to encourage food sharing and asked people to bring a dish or some snacks to work for lunch on certain days, place everything on a big central table – and then invite everyone to help themselves. The lunches that followed were wonderful – people talked not only about their own dishes, but had a chance to share other people's cooking and learn about their colleague's food heritage. It was a different way of connecting because the food was homemade and it was made with love: it was made for sharing. Those were the most hyggelige lunches.

Hygge and food go together. Setting the scene for creating a hyggelig atmosphere usually involves some kind of food. Perhaps a brunch for friends after a night out. Afternoon fika with the neighbour over a cup of tea and a warm bun. Catching up with your mum and a cookie or two. When we give our time and our love and we share the moment, hygge magically appears between us and allows us to

forget about the world outside. We remove the outside from the equation by ignoring it, putting the phone in a different room and not watching the news. In hygge, there are no politics, no dangers, no sadness. Only appreciating the people you are sharing the moment with, right there and then. It may only be a lunch break, it may only be afternoon fika – but in those pockets of time, both bellies and hearts feel full.

SAFFRON BUNDT CAKE WITH PEARS

Saffran och päronkaka

30 g/¼ cup breadcrumbs

50 g/3½ tablespoons butter

100 ml/⅓ cup plus 1 tablespoon whole milk

0.5 g/½ teaspoon ground saffron

2 large or 3 small pears

a little lemon juice

325 g/1½ cups plus 2 tablespoons caster/granulated sugar

4 eggs

300 g/2¼ cups plain/all-purpose flour

2 teaspoons baking powder

1 teaspoon vanilla extract

½ teaspoon of salt

50 g/¼ cup Greek yogurt

icing/confectioners' sugar, for dusting

a 25-cm/9-in. Bundt pan or ring pan, greased

SERVES 10

Across Scandinavia in December you will likely be offered a saffron-flavoured Lucia bun in honour of the Feast of St Lucia. I also make this beautiful, light saffron cake with pears.

Preheat the oven to 180°C (350°F) Gas 4.

Dust the greased Bundt or ring pan with the breadcrumbs, tipping out the excess.

Melt the butter and add the milk and ground saffron. Stir to combine and set aside to infuse.

Peel and core the pears and cut into bite-sized chunks. Add a dash of lemon juice, stir and set aside.

In a mixing bowl, beat the sugar and eggs until thick, light and fluffy using a balloon whisk or a hand-held electric whisk. Mix the remaining dry ingredients together and sift into the egg mixture. Fold in until incorporated. Add the Greek yogurt and saffron-milk mixture and fold gently until completely combined. Pour the cake batter into the prepared Bundt pan. Add the pieces of pear – these will sink down during baking.

Bake for around 30–35 minutes in the preheated oven or until a skewer inserted into the middle comes out clean. Leave to cool in the pan before turning out onto a serving tray. Dust with icing/confectioners' sugar and serve, sliced, with a good dollop of whipped cream.

DANISH DREAM CAKE

Drømmekage fra Brovst

This Danish Dream Cake originates from Brovst, in Jutland. In 1965, a young girl baked her secret family recipe in a competition and won, and the cake has been a favourite of all Danes ever since. No wonder: it's light and fluffy with a delicious coconut topping.

3 eggs

225 g/1 cup caster/ granulated sugar

$^1/_2$ teaspoon vanilla sugar

225 g/1$^3/_4$ cups plain/ all-purpose flour or cake flour

2 teaspoons baking powder

150 ml/$^2/_3$ cup whole milk

75 g/$^3/_4$ stick butter, melted

TOPPING:

100 g/1 stick butter

150 g/1$^1/_2$ cups desiccated/ dried shredded coconut

250 g/1$^1/_4$ cups dark brown sugar

75 ml/$^1/_3$ cup whole milk

a pinch of salt

a 23-cm/9-in. springform or round cake pan, greased and lined with baking parchment

SERVES 10–12

Preheat the oven to 190°C (375°F) Gas 5.

In the bowl of a food mixer, whisk the eggs, caster/ granulated sugar and vanilla sugar on a high speed for a few minutes, until white and light. Meanwhile, in a separate bowl, sift the flour and baking powder together.

Carefully fold the flour into the egg mixture. Mix the milk with the melted butter in a jug/pitcher and carefully pour into the batter, folding it in until incorporated. Pour the batter into the prepared cake pan.

Bake in the preheated oven for 35–40 minutes, or until almost done (try not to open the oven door for the first 20 minutes of the total baking time).

To make the topping, put all the ingredients in a saucepan and gently melt together.

Remove the cake from the oven and carefully spread the topping all over the cake. Return to the oven. Turn up the heat to 200°C (400°F) Gas 6 and bake for a further 5 minutes.

Leave cake to cool before eating, if you can (we are well aware it's hard to do that).

APPLE AND CINNAMON CAKE

Æblekage med kanel

150 g/1¼ sticks butter

200 g/1 cup caster/
granulated sugar

1 teaspoon vanilla sugar
or extract

4 eggs

200 g/1½ cups plain/
all-purpose flour or
cake flour

½ teaspoon salt

1½ teaspoons baking
powder

150 g/¾ cup Crème
Pâtissière (see page 74)

pouring cream, to serve
(optional)

continued over page

There a many different kinds of 'Real Scandinavian' Apple Cakes out there. Truth be told, there are as many 'real recipes' for apple cakes as there are people who bake them. This is a cake my mother used to bake when I was a kid, using apples from the garden. At the café, we added a layer of crème pâtissière to it for a bit of extra scrumptiousness. This is one of the most popular cakes at the café.

First, make the topping. In a saucepan, melt together the butter, sugar and cinnamon and add the salt and vanilla extract. Add the chopped apple and stew for a few minutes to lightly start the cooking process, then take off the heat and allow to cool completely. This can be done a day in advance.

Preheat the oven to 175°C (350°F) Gas 4.

To make the cake, cream the butter, caster/granulated sugar and vanilla sugar or extract together in a bowl until pale and fluffy. Lightly beat the eggs in a separate bowl, then add to the butter and sugar mixture in three stages, whisking all the time. Ensure that all the egg is fully incorporated before adding more or the batter will curdle.

continued from previous page

TOPPING:

25 g/2 tablespoons butter

**50 g/¹/₄ cup caster/
granulated sugar**

**2 teaspoons ground
cinnamon**

a sprinkling of sea salt

¹/₂ teaspoon vanilla extract

**3 Granny Smith apples,
peeled, cored and chopped
into 1-cm/¹/₂-in. cubes**

*a 23-cm/9-in. springform or
round cake pan, greased and
lined with baking parchment*

SERVES 8–10

In a third bowl, combine the flour, salt and baking powder. Sift into the wet mixture and carefully fold in until fully incorporated.

Pour the mixture into the prepared cake pan and spread evenly to the sides. Dollop the crème pâtissière on top and spread out evenly over the batter.

Using a slotted spoon, remove the apple from its syrup and scatter over the crème pâtissière. Reserve the syrup for drizzling over the cake once baked.

Bake in the preheated oven for around 50 minutes – it can be tricky to tell if the cake is done because the crème pâtissière will remain a bit wet, but if a skewer comes out clean, it should be baked inside.

Remove from the pan and allow to cool slightly before eating.

Enjoy with cream, if you so wish – and pour over some of the leftover syrup for added oomph (I like to add a little more salt to the syrup – it really lifts it).

chapter 4

HYGGE AND... BAKING

*A party without cake
is just a meeting.*

JULIA CHILD

It's fair to say I grew up next to the oven.

As a lover of all baked goods, I was never far from a batch of freshly baked deliciousness – and the local baker quite likely had to wash his window daily from the imprint of my sticky face trying to get a closer look at the cakes on my way home from school. As soon as I was old enough to be allowed to turn on the oven, I was baking, sharing my cakes and breads with whoever wanted to help me eat them.

Over the years, I've come to realise that baking can be a form of solace as much as it is a place of hygge and comfort. Like a sorcerer, potions are conjured up in the kitchen by combining ingredients in just the right order. Baking, to me, is different to just cooking – it requires concentration, precision and an emotional investment all at the same time. If you do not add love to baking, I truly don't think it works the same way. On top of that, no two people's cakes taste the same, even if the ingredients list is identical.

To me, one of the most hyggelige things I can think of is when I bake with my kids. We spend afternoons in our warm kitchen that smells of vanilla and cinnamon and is full of love. To me, there is no better place on earth.

I once asked one of my daughters why she loves baking so much – apart from getting to lick the bowl and eat brownies straight out of the oven – and she answered: 'Because we talk all the time when we bake. And baking is like, magic; things spring to life'. She's right – we really talk in the kitchen, about everything and nothing. It doesn't matter that the kitchen usually ends up being splattered with melted chocolate or that the results are often wonky – to me, those cakes are the best in the world and there are no better way to connect with my children than when we make magic in the kitchen.

There is a common purpose as you dance with someone else in a kitchen, creating all things sweet and delicious. What we learn there helps shape us as people, too. The science of baking teaches us attention to detail, as well as patience, alongside the obvious chemistry lesson. Connecting with others not only through the act of the baking itself but also carrying this over into the sharing of the food afterwards. Hygge with home baking? Yes, please – I'll take that any day over even the fanciest store-bought cake. Because the best cakes taste of love.

BIRTHDAY BUNS
Fødselsdagsboller

200 ml/³/₄ cup whole milk

50 ml/3¹/₂ tablespoons single/light cream

25 g/1 oz. fresh yeast or 13 g/2¹/₂ teaspoons dried/active dry yeast

50 g/¹/₄ cup caster/granulated sugar

400 g/3 cups white strong/bread flour

1 teaspoon salt

1 egg

80 g/³/₄ stick butter, softened

beaten egg, for brushing

a baking sheet, greased and lined with baking parchment

MAKES 12

continued over page

My farmor (grandmother) Inger used to bake these for us on birthdays and treat days. After running around in the cold getting rosy cheeks, we'd head back into the warm house for one of these sweet buns. We'd eat them with so much butter our teeth would leave an indent (this phenomenon is known as tandsmør – literally meaning tooth butter!). In Denmark, these birthday buns are traditionally arranged in the shape of a stick man or woman, then baked and decorated with icing and wine gum mouths, liquorice eyes and gummy laces for hair.

Mix together the milk and cream and heat to finger-warm (around 36–37°C/97–98°F).

If using fresh yeast, add the yeast and warmed milk-cream to a stand mixer with a dough hook attached. Mix until the yeast has dissolved. If using dried/active dry yeast pour the warmed milk and cream into a bowl. Sprinkle on the yeast and whisk together. Cover with clingfilm/plastic wrap and leave in a warm place for about 15 minutes to activate and become frothy. Pour into the stand mixer with a dough hook.

Add the caster/granulated sugar and stir again, slowly adding half the flour mixed with the salt, bit by bit. Add the egg and softened butter and keep mixing. Slowly add

continued from previous page

the other half of the flour. You may not need all the flour or you may need a bit more, but keep mixing until you have a slightly sticky dough that is starting to let go of the sides of the bowl. This should take around 5–7 minutes.

Cover the bowl with clingfilm/plastic wrap and leave to rise for around 35–40 minutes or until doubled in size.

Turn the dough out onto a lightly floured surface and knead through with your hands, adding only a little more flour if needed.

Cut the dough into 12 equal pieces and roll them into uniformly round balls. Place on the prepared baking sheet. Cover again and leave to rise for a further 20 minutes.

Preheat the oven to 200°C (400°F) Gas 6.

Brush each bun lightly with beaten egg, then bake in the preheated oven for around 10–12 minutes or until golden brown.

Remove from the oven and place a damp, clean kitchen cloth on top for a few minutes if you prefer the buns without a hard crust. Serve sliced open, with butter or some Scandinavian sliced cheese.

SEEDED RYE ROLLS

Rugbøller

100 g/¹/₂ cup chopped rye kernels/rye berries

100 g/³/₄ cup sunflower seeds (save 50 g/¹/₃ cup for topping)

100 g/³/₄ cup pumpkin seeds (save 50g/¹/₃ cup for topping)

50 g/¹/₄ cup flaxseeds/linseeds

13 g/2¹/₂ teaspoons dried/active dry yeast or 25 g/1 oz. fresh yeast *(see page 58)

100 ml/7 tablespoons finger-warm water (36–37°C/ 97–98°F)

250 ml/1 cup buttermilk

4 teaspoons vegetable oil

2 teaspoons salt

2 teaspoons barley malt syrup

200 g/1¹/₂ cups wholegrain rye flour

continued over page

Scandinavians do love bread rolls in the morning, especially the Danes. I make these at home a lot on weekends for breakfast for my family. We freeze leftover rolls and use them for packed lunches, too, as the kids love them (and frankly, any excuse to avoid mass-produced bread). Lots of seeds and rye kernels give these rolls a nice healthy edge, but the mixture of wheat and rye ensures the rolls stay soft. Try filling these rolls with smoked salmon and cream cheese.

Place the rye kernels/rye berries, sunflower seeds, pumpkin seeds and flaxseeds/linseeds in a saucepan. Cover with water, bring to the boil and allow to boil for a few minutes. Pour into a sieve/strainer, run cold water through to cool, then press out the excess water.

If using dried/active dry yeast, pour the finger-warm water into a bowl, sprinkle on the yeast and whisk. Cover with clingfilm/plastic wrap and leave in a warm place for 15 minutes to activate.

Gently warm the buttermilk to finger-warm. Pour the buttermilk and yeast into a mixing bowl. Add the oil, salt and syrup and stir, then add all the rye flour and mix well. Add the rye kernels/rye berries and seeds, then slowly start adding the strong/bread flour (you may not need to add all of it). Keep kneading for about 5 minutes in a machine

continued from previous page

500 g/3½ cups white
strong/ bread flour (hold
back a bit)

egg or water, for brushing

*2 baking sheets, greased and
lined with baking parchment*

MAKES 18

*If using fresh yeast, add it
to the water and buttermilk
and stir to dissolve.

(longer if by hand). The dough should be a bit sticky, but
stretchy. Cover the bowl with clingfilm/plastic wrap or
a dish towel and leave to rise for about 1 hour or until it
has doubled in size.

On a floured surface, tip out the dough and knead it
through. Make sure it is nice and elastic at this stage –
if not, add a bit more flour. Using your hands or a rolling
pin, roll the dough to a 20 x 45-cm/8 x 17-in. rectangle.
Carefully move the dough to one side, spread one-third
of the reserved seeds on the table and lay the dough back
over. Lightly brush the surface with egg or water, scatter
the remaining seeds on top and press gently into the
dough. Using a dough or pizza cutter, cut the rectangle
into 18 equal squares.

Preheat the oven to 180°C (350°F) Gas 4.

Place the rolls (well spread out) on the baking sheets. Leave
to rise again for 20 minutes, covered with clingfilm/plastic
wrap. Bake for around 15 minutes. Remove from the oven
and leave to cool.

SWEDISH SCONES

Svenska scones

200 g/1½ cups wholemeal/ wholegrain spelt flour

250 g/1¾ cups plus 2 tablespoons plain/ all-purpose flour

4 teaspoons baking powder

1 teaspoon salt

125 g/1⅛ sticks butter, cubed

200 ml/¾ cup whole milk

150 g/¾ cup Greek yogurt, skyr or filmjölk or similar soured or strained milk

1 tablespoon golden/light corn syrup

beaten egg or milk, for brushing

butter and or mild Scandinavian cheese, to serve

2 baking sheets, greased and lined with baking parchment

MAKES 16

I often make these Swedish scones if I don't have bread in the house, they take just a few minutes to put together and not long to bake. Swedes refer to these as *Svenska* scones, but the basis for them is actually more akin to making soda bread.

Preheat the oven to 200°C (400°F) Gas 6.

In a bowl, combine the flours, baking powder and salt. Mix in the cubed butter with your hands until the mixture is grainy and even. Add the milk, yogurt and syrup and combine with the flour and butter. Mix lightly until you have an even, grainy dough. Don't knead it.

Cut the dough into 4 even pieces and roll each one into a ball. Flatten the balls to discs of around 15–16 cm/ 6–6¼ in. in diameter. Cut a cross almost all the way through on each disc.

Arrange on the prepared baking sheets and brush with beaten egg or milk. Bake in the preheated oven for 15–18 minutes or until golden brown, well-risen and baked through. Leave to cool slightly before breaking each disc into 4 along the scored lines.

Slice open to serve. Best eaten on day of baking.

This recipe is quite forgiving – you can vary the flour you use to suit your taste (although if you use lots of rye or coarse wholemeal/wholegrain, you will need to add a bit of extra liquid or plain/all-purpose flour). I also sometimes add seeds or even grated carrots to the mixture.

chapter 5

HYGGE AND... DARKNESS

*Better to light a candle than
to curse the darkness.*

CHINESE PROVERB

Scandinavian houses are often portrayed as being full of candles.

It is true: we burn more candles than most nations put together. You only have to look at the extensive candle selection in Ikea to see how seriously we take candle lighting in our homes. Enter any Scandinavian home and you are guaranteed to find that as soon as darkness falls, candles are lit – and not just a few.

The darkness that sets over Scandinavia when autumn/fall comes instills a feeling of wanting to hibernate and large parts of the region have little or no light for half of the year. The further north you go, the quicker the darkness envelopes the landscape, even months before the snow comes. You wake to darkness and return home from work in darkness. For most, this would be a fast-forward to depression. Scandinavians do suffer from their fair share of seasonal mood disorders – but compared to how dark and cold it is, it is relative: we have learnt to make darkness part of our lives and we live along, and inside, it and embrace it as best we can.

In years gone by, farms were required to have a light by the door of the house so that passers-by could find their dwellings in darkness and storms. Even today, during the darkest months, we put candles and small lamps at our windows. During December, all houses have

little electric candle bridges of seven lights in most windows, or big paper stars.

Nordic darkness can be tough to live through, year after year. We find our little ways of coping, and these little guiding lights are part of that. Light creates atmosphere, and atmosphere can help to create hygge, which is why you see so many people illustrating hygge by lighting a bunch of candles. Every bit of darkness is instantly broken by even a tiny glimmer of light – and the tiniest spec of light can sometimes feel the warmest and brightest of all.

That said, you can light as many candles as you like and not feel hygge – the candles do not make the feeling on their own. Candles can, however, elevate hygge and hurry it along because they help to set the scene. Rarely is darkness a frantic place of hustle and bustle, but rather a place of calm and reflection. While the darkness itself is cold, fireplaces and candles are warm. Hygge is a warm feeling that grows well in a dimly lit room.

You only have to look at the front covers of many of the books about hygge to see that candles, fireplaces and blankets are often associated with hygge. These things alone are not hygge. But there are many conscious things that we might chose to do in order to set the scene, and a lot of these things do tend to happen in the slower months, especially around Christmas. Admittedly, these do include lighting candles and log fires (if you are lucky enough to have one) and quite likely baking cookies or cinnamon buns or similar – definitely a warming treat of some sort.

There is nothing wrong with setting a scene for when you want to hygge, alone or with others. It is all about doing things that make you feel relaxed and this may well be lighting candles. If you are with friends, maybe play some good music or open a bottle of delicious wine. If you are alone, wear pants with an elasticated waistband, eat a box of chocolates and watch 'Love Actually' on the TV. However, always keep in mind the objective of the event, and perhaps resist inviting people over to hygge with you wearing their slippers – it may not be their idea of fun and hygge isn't some sort of party séance.

Hygge happens sometimes, and sometimes not. Just as you can't guarantee you will have a great time at a party, there is no guarantee that you will experience a feeling of hygge every time you light a fire or put on a pair of cosy socks. On the other hand, you may get back from a disappointing party, put on those comfortable pants and open a special bottle of something with your partner or room mate – and hygge is quite possibly hiding in there.

REAL CINNAMON BUNS

Kanelbullar

DOUGH:

13 g/2^1/$_2$ teaspoons dried/
active dry yeast or 25 g/1 oz.
fresh yeast

250 ml/1 cup whole milk,
heated to 36–37°C
(97–99°F)

80 g/^{3}/$_4$ stick butter, melted
and cooled slightly

40 g/3 tablespoons caster/
granulated sugar

400–500 g/3–3^2/$_3$ cups
white strong/bread flour

2 teaspoons ground
cardamom

1 teaspoon salt

1 egg, beaten

continued over page

Having a good recipe for *kanelbullar* is essential,
because it's the Scandi treat you will make over and
over. Don't forget to knead some love into the dough;
it makes them extra-delicious.

If using fresh yeast, add the warm milk to a mixing bowl
and add the yeast; stir until dissolved, then pour into the
bowl of the food mixer. If using dried/active dry yeast, pour
the warm milk into a bowl, sprinkle in the yeast and whisk
together. Cover with clingfilm/plastic wrap and leave in a
warm place for about 15 minutes to become bubbly. Pour
into the bowl of a food mixer fitted with a dough hook.

Mix in the cooled, melted butter. Allow to combine for
1 minute or so, then add the sugar. In a separate bowl,
weigh out 400 g/3 cups of the flour, add the cardamom
and salt and mix. Start adding the flour and spices into
the milk mixture, bit by bit. Add half the beaten egg. Keep
kneading for 5 minutes. You may need to add more flour
– you want the mixture to end up a bit sticky. It is better
not to add too much flour as this will result in dry buns.
You can always add more later.

Cover the dough with clingfilm/plastic wrap. Allow to rise
for around 30 minutes or until it has doubled in size.

continued from previous page

FILLING:

**80 g/¹/₂ stick plus
1 tablespoon butter, at room
temperature**

**1 teaspoon plain/all-purpose
flour**

**1 tablespoon ground
cinnamon**

**¹/₂ teaspoon ground
cardamom**

¹/₂ teaspoon vanilla sugar

**80 g/¹/₄ cup plus
2 tablespoons caster/
granulated sugar**

beaten egg, for brushing

TOPPING:

**3 tablespoons golden/light
corn syrup (warmed) and
nibbed 'pearl' sugar**

*2 baking sheets, greased and
lined with baking parchment*

MAKES 16

Turn the dough out onto a lightly floured surface. Knead through with your hands and work in more flour if needed. Roll out the dough to a 40 x 50 cm/16 x 20 in. rectangle.

In a bowl, add the butter, flour, spices and sugars and mix together well to make the filling. Using a spatula, spread the mixture evenly over the rolled-out dough. Fold the dough in half lengthways.

Using a knife or pizza cutter, cut 16 widthways strips of dough. Take one strip and carefully twist it a few times, then curl into a 'knot', ensuring both ends are tucked in or under so they do not spring open during baking. Place the folded 'knots' on the prepared baking sheets spaced well apart. Leave to rise under a kitchen cloth for 30 minutes.

Preheat the oven to 200°C (400°F) Gas 6.

Brush each bun lightly with beaten egg and place in the preheated oven to bake for around 10–12 minutes or until golden.

Remove from the oven. Brush the warm buns lightly with syrup then decorate with the nibbed 'pearl' sugar. Immediately cover with a damp, clean cloth for a few minutes to prevent the buns from going dry.

1 x 75-cl/26-fl. oz. bottle red wine (the quality doesn't matter)

1–2 cinnamon sticks

1 teaspoon dried root ginger

1 teaspoon dried Seville orange peel (or other orange peel if you can't get Seville)

7 whole cardamom pods

15–16 whole cloves

80 g/$\frac{1}{3}$ cup plus 1 tablespoon caster/granulated sugar

flaked/slivered almonds and raisins, to serve

SERVES 4

GLÖGG

Nordic mulled wine

Glögg is an essential part of Christmas all over Scandinavia. It's enjoyed throughout the cold months and especially on Sundays in Advent leading up to Christmas. Glögg tends to be traditionally mulled with cinnamon, cardamom, cloves and dried orange peel. This is recipe is borrowed from my sister-in-law Annika, who makes bottles and bottles of this in her Gothenburg kitchen every December.

Pour the wine into a saucepan, add the rest of the ingredients and heat to around 75–80°C (165–170°F), stirring to dissolve the sugar. Be careful not to heat it above 80°C (170°F) degrees, or the alcohol will start to evaporate. Remove the saucepan from the heat and leave to infuse for at least 1 hour, longer if possible.

Strain the mixture and return the mulled wine to the bottle (use a funnel to make life easier for yourself). The Glögg can be kept for at least a week.

To serve, pour the wine into a saucepan and heat it up (again, take care not to let it boil). Place a few flaked/slivered almonds and raisins in the bottom of your serving cups, and pour the Glögg over the mixture.

If you want to give your Glögg an extra kick, add a splash of either vodka, aquavit, rum or cognac to the bottom of the cups just before you pour in the Glögg.

NORWEGIAN CREAM BUNS
Skoleboller

DOUGH:

13 g/2^1/$_2$ teaspoons dried/
active dry yeast or 25 g/1 oz.
fresh yeast *(see page 74)

250 ml/1 cup whole milk,
heated to 36–37°C
(97–99°F)

80 g/^{3}/$_4$ stick butter, melted
and cooled slightly

40 g/3 tablespoons caster/
granulated sugar

400–500 g/3–3^2/$_3$ cups
white strong/bread flour

2 teaspoons ground
cardamom

1 teaspoon salt

1 egg, beaten

continued over page

This is the ultimate comfort bun for Norwegians. Traditionally named 'Skoleboller' ('school buns'), we call them Norwegian cream buns at the café.

Pour the warm milk into a bowl, sprinkle in the yeast and whisk together. Cover with clingfilm/plastic wrap and leave in a warm place for about 15 minutes to become bubbly. Pour into the bowl of a food mixer fitted with a dough hook. Start the machine and add the cooled, melted butter. Allow to combine with the yeast for 1 minute or so, then add the sugar. Allow to combine for 1 minute.

In a separate bowl, weigh out 400 g/3 cups of the flour, add the cardamom and salt and mix together. Start adding the flour and spices into the milk mixture, bit by bit. Add half the beaten egg. Keep kneading for 5 minutes. You may need to add more flour – you want the mixture to end up a bit sticky, but not so much that it sticks to your finger if you poke it. It is better not to add too much flour as this will result in dry buns. You can always add more later.

Once mixed, leave the dough in a bowl and cover with a dish towel or clingfilm/plastic wrap. Allow to rise for around 30 minutes or until it has doubled in size.

continued from previous page

TOPPING & BRUSHING:

1 beaten egg, for brushing

150 g/1 cup icing/
confectioners' sugar

50 g/²/₃ cup desiccated/
dried shredded coconut

CRÈME PÂTISSIÈRE:

500 ml/2 cups whole milk

¹/₂ vanilla pod/bean

2 eggs

100 g/¹/₂ cup caster/
granulated sugar

30 g/¹/₄ cup cornflour/
cornstarch

¹/₂ teaspoon salt

25 g/2 tablespoons butter

MAKES 14

*If using fresh yeast, add the
warm milk to a mixing bowl
and add the yeast; stir until
dissolved, then pour into the
bowl of the food mixer.

Meanwhile, make the Crème Pâtissière. Heat the milk in a saucepan together with the scraped out vanilla seeds. Add the whole pod/bean to the pan, too, for extra flavour.

In a bowl, whisk together the eggs, sugar, cornflour/cornstarch and salt. When the milk reaches boiling point, remove the vanilla pod/bean and discard, and pour a quarter of the hot milk into the egg mixture, whisking as you do so. Once whisked through, pour the egg mixture back into the remaining hot milk, return to the heat and bring to the boil, whisking continuously. Let it bubble for just under a minute. Make sure you whisk as it thickens.

Remove from the heat and add the butter, whisking in well. Pour into a cold bowl, then cover the top with a sheet of baking parchment to prevent a hard edge from forming as it cools down. Place in the fridge to cool completely.

After the dough has risen, roll out the dough into a cylinder and cut it into 14 pieces. Roll each piece into a neat circle, then place on a baking sheet and flatten firmly (although they will spring back into place after a while). Make sure you space the buns out evenly.

Using the base of a glass measuring around 4–5 cm/1¹/₂–2 in. in diameter, press down the middle of each bun and add a good tablespoon of Crème Pâtissière to each indentation.

Leave the buns to rise for a further 20 minutes.

Preheat the oven to 200°C (400°F) Gas 6.

Lightly brush the buns with egg (avoid the custard centres) and bake in the preheated oven for around 10 minutes, or until done (times may vary depending on your oven).

Cover the baked buns with a damp dish towel for 5–10 minutes as soon as you have removed them from the oven to avoid a crust forming.

Once the buns have cooled, make the icing/frosting. Add a few tablespoons of hot water to the icing/confectioners' sugar and stir. Keep adding water, drop by drop, and stirring until you have a smooth consistency that can be stirred but is still thick, like a syrup.

Using a plastic pastry brush or a palette knife, carefully smooth the icing/frosting on top of all the buns, avoiding the cream centre.

After each bun has been brushed, sprinkle coconut over the top.

NORDIC GINGER BISCUITS

Pepparkakor

550 g/4 cups plain/
all-purpose flour

1 teaspoon bicarbonate of/
baking soda

1 teaspoon ground ginger

1 teaspoon ground cloves

2 teaspoons ground
cinnamon

1 teaspoon ground
cardamom

pinch of ground allspice

pinch of salt

150 g/1 stick plus 2
tablespoons butter, at room
temperature

200 g/10 tablespoons
golden/light corn syrup

100 g/$\frac{1}{2}$ cup granulated
sugar

100 g/$\frac{1}{2}$ cup dark brown
sugar

150 ml/$\frac{1}{2}$ cup double/
heavy cream

$\frac{1}{2}$ teaspoon orange zest

icing/confectioners' sugar,
to dust

MAKES 50–70

It's not Christmas without each Scandinavian person consuming a mountain of these biscuits! It's such fun to make these with the kids, and really get into the festive mood together.

Mix the flour and bicarbonate of/baking soda with the dry spices and salt. Add the butter and all the other ingredients and mix until you have an even dough. It may still be sticky, but shape into a log and wrap in clingfilm/plastic wrap and leave to rest in the fridge overnight before using. Try to resist eating the dough every time you pass by the fridge. Yes, we know it is hard not to do!

Preheat the oven to 200°C (400°F) Gas 6.

Roll out the dough thinly on a floured surface and use cookie cutters to cut your desired shapes. You want the biscuits/cookies to be thin.

Bake in the preheated oven on lined baking sheets – each batch will take 5–6 minutes depending on the thickness. You want the biscuits/cookies to be a darker shade of brown.

Remove from the oven and cool on a cooling rack. Dust with icing/confectioners' sugar and serve or keep in an airtight container.

chapter 6

HYGGE AND... LIGHT

*Just living is not enough...
one must have sunshine,
freedom, and a little flower.*

HANS CHRISTIAN ANDERSEN

We are so lucky in Scandinavia.

As a pay-off for making it through those long dark months, we get the ultimate light in the summer. In some places, the sun doesn't set for several weeks over Midsummer and we go a bit doolally trying to get to sleep when every fibre of our being just wants to be awake and out doing stuff. Sitting outside at almost midnight with no extra light to help you read your book is an extraordinary experience and one we treasure and appreciate greatly.

Every Scandinavian knows you can hygge as easily in the summer as you can in the winter. There are no specific seasons for hygge, although the media outside Scandinavia has found it easier to illustrate hygge by showing people wearing thick socks, burning hundreds of candles and generally wearing sweaters indoors (Scandinavians don't often wear sweaters indoors, by the way – houses are well insulated and our sweaters are knitted with thick wool).

Hygge in the light is all about nature and being outside. Once the sun is out, wild horses couldn't keep us inside. Well, it is only natural when half your year is dark and cold that you appreciate the lighter days all the more.

All Scandinavians love the outdoors – from the super-active to the 'I just want to sit in my garden' people – from May until September, you will find few Scandinavians indoors unless they have something essential to do there. Having a very limited summer season really does mean we make as much use of it as we can.

A lot of Scandinavians have summer houses. These range from allotments with little huts (people do sometimes stay in these, too) to wooden huts in the mountains (the Norwegian hytte) to Swedish red cottages by the lakes and Danish beach houses. What all these have in common is the lack of facilities compared to our winter houses. Quite a few Norwegian holiday 'hytter' don't even have toilets, just outhouses.

Denmark as a country is so small that everything is connected up, but a lot of people don't bring their TV with them to their beach house anyway, nor do they re-route their wifi for the duration of their trip. This is because summer cottages are all about going back to basics – and back to nature – and about making time and space to hygge with friends and family.

Hygge in the light is about being near your cottage, going for long walks, swimming in the lakes or the sea or even playing Monopoly and eating canned spaghetti with ketchup. It's about sharing ice creams on the beach. It's baking a cake with summer berries from the garden and sharing it with the neighbour for fika. It's foraging for mushrooms and then cooking your loot over an open fire and serving on buttered toast. All of these things are often done with loved ones, and without a smartphone or the need to Instagram every precious moment. It's about taking time to go back to basics and doing the things that makes you feel wholesome again. Not a woolly sock in sight and still maximizing all the hygge buttons by just appreciating the lighter days together.

Hygge in the summer is making a den with the kids under some trees, then sitting in there while the rain pours down outside, sharing a packet of crisps/chips. Hygge is there in a tent with you, because you are warm and your fancy construction worked and didn't take in water – the world outside is wet and rainy, but you are dry (and so are your snacks). The contents of that packet are the best you have ever tasted because you know the kids will always remember that moment.

SMOKED MACKEREL WITH FENNEL AND APPLE OPEN SANDWICH

Makrel & Æble

100 g/3½ oz. green peas, defrosted

2 teaspoons chopped chives

1 teaspoon chopped tarragon

lemon juice

drop of olive oil

salt and freshly ground black pepper

2 slices of buttered dark seeded rye bread

1 large smoked mackerel fillet

¼ fennel bulb

¼ green apple

sprigs of dill, to garnish

SERVES 2

Our friend Kobi came up with this open sandwich. We just love the crunch from the fennel and apple – it works so well with the delicious smoked mackerel. This open sandwich really does work best on dark seeded rye bread. It is one of the most popular recipes at the café – and a perfect summery open sandwich.

Using a fork, crush the peas in a bowl, then add the chives and tarragon, a few drops of lemon juice and olive oil. Mix together and season with salt and pepper.

Place each slice of bread on serving plate. Add the crushed pea mixture and spread evenly.

Remove the skin from the smoked mackerel fillet and place a generous piece on top of the pea mixture (usually, around half a fillet is big enough, but this depends on personal preference).

Finely shave the fennel using a mandolin (or with a super sharp knife) and place in a bowl. Then shave the apple the same way. Combine the apple with the fennel and dress with few more drops of lemon juice, olive oil (optional) and seasoning, if needed. Spoon on top of the mackerel, garnish with dill and serve.

Note: See overleaf for the roast beef and prawn/shrimp toppings.

EGG AND PRAWN/SHRIMP

Æg & Rejer

butter

2 slices of dark rye bread

3 hard-boiled/cooked eggs

1/4 teaspoon Dijon mustard

1 tablespoon mayonnaise

1 tablespoon chopped chives

salt and freshly ground black pepper

2–4 slices of tomato

2 small handfuls of high-quality peeled prawns/shrimp

sprigs of dill, to garnish

lemon juice

SERVES 2

You will be offered the classic egg and prawn open sandwich (photo on page 85) across Scandinavia. We have updated it slightly with a delicious egg salad.

Butter the bread and arrange on serving plates.

Roughly chop the eggs and mix with the mustard, mayonnaise and chives. Season to taste.

Add a few slices of tomato to the bread, then spoon the egg mixture on top. Arrange the prawns on top of the egg salad, then decorate with a sprig of dill and a squeeze of lemon.

ROAST BEEF AND CRISPY ONIONS

Roastbof & Ristedeløg

This is the classic Danish open sandwich (photo on page 85) and one of the most popular. You will find it on the menu at every restaurant or deli and in our homes.

To make crispy onions, if using shallots, cut them into rings; if using a large onion, cut it into quarters, then slice finely. Put the flour, salt and pepper into a plastic bag, add the onions and shake until they are coated. Discard excess flour.

Heat the vegetable oil in a small saucepan to 130–140°C (approx. 280°F). If the temperature is too hot, the onions will burn; if it's too cold, they will be soggy.

Once the oil reaches frying temperature, add a third of the onion or 1 shallot to the oil and cook until golden brown. Remove with a slotted spoon and leave to drain on paper towels. Repeat with the other two batches. Allow to cool slightly before using so they crisp up.

Lightly butter the rye bread and arrange on serving plates. Arrange the lettuce on the bread and then fold the roast beef neatly on top in sections. You want to try to create a bit of height to the sandwich to make it look really appetizing. This is easiest to do with very thinly sliced beef.

Next, add the remoulade dressing in the middle, cut the cherry tomatoes in half and arrange on the remoulade. Grate the horseradish to taste and add the 1 tablespoon of the Crispy Onions. Garnish with a sprig of chervil.

butter

2 slices of dark seeded rye bread

2 green salad leaves

8 very thin slices of rare roast beef (cold) – about 60 g/2 oz. per sandwich

2 tablespoons Danish Remoulade

2 cherry tomatoes

freshly grated horseradish, to taste

chervil sprig, to garnish

CRISPY ONIONS (MAKES ENOUGH FOR 6–8 SANDWICHES):

1 large sweet onion or 3 shallots

1 tablespoon plain/all-purpose flour

salt and freshly ground black pepper

150 ml/$^1/_2$ cup plus 1 tablespoon vegetable oil, for frying

SERVES 2

BISCUIT BASES:

300 g/2¼ cups plain/all-purpose flour

2 egg yolks

175 g/1½ sticks butter

2 tablespoons double/heavy cream

25 g/1 oz. icing/confectioners' sugar

½ teaspoon grated lemon zest

MERINGUE TOPPING:

2 egg whites

a tiny pinch of salt

275 g/1½ cups minus 2 tablespoons caster/superfine sugar

1 teaspoon vanilla sugar OR extract OR the seeds from 1 vanilla pod/bean

1 teaspoon white wine vinegar

3 tablespoons finely chopped almonds

a baking sheet, greased and lined with baking parchment

a 5-cm/1-in. fluted pastry/cookie cutter

a piping/pastry bag fitted with a star nozzle/tip

MAKES 30–35

NOTHING BISCUITS

Ingenting

This treat is called Ingenting – which means 'nothing'. Because when people say 'I can eat nothing more', you can always fit in one of these very light treats!

Blitz the ingredients for the biscuit bases briefly in a food processor. Once a smooth dough has formed, wrap in clingfilm/plastic wrap and chill in the refrigerator for at least 30 minutes.

Preheat the oven to 160°C (300°F) Gas 2.

Roll out the dough on a lightly floured surface to a thickness of 3 mm/⅛ in. Using the round fluted pastry/cookie cutter, stamp out circles and place on the prepared baking sheet. Repeat until all the dough has been used.

For the meringue topping, beat the egg whites with a tiny pinch of salt until stiff using a hand-held electric whisk or in a stand mixer with the whisk attachment. Slowly add the sugar and vanilla, bit by bit, and whisk on high speed until you have a shiny mixture that forms stiff peaks (still soft enough to be spoon-able). Fold in the vinegar and chopped almonds.

Pipe or spoon the meringue mixture onto each biscuit base, spreading or placing it almost to the edge (the meringue will not spread much during baking).

Bake the biscuits in the middle of the preheated oven for around 18–20 minutes or until the base is cooked and the top is lightly browned. Remove from the oven and allow to cool before eating.

chapter 7

HYGGE AND... TIME

Time is a created thing.
To say 'I don't have Time,'
is like saying
'I don't want to'.

LAO TZU

My grandmother had the most hyggelige kitchen in the world.

It was a huge, old white house, situated on the outskirts of the village. It had creaky floorboards in the hallway and lots of great hiding places in the loft. It wasn't very stylish and it was full of old people's stuff, like most grandparents' houses should be. Inside every nook and cranny the house was filled with love. So full of love and warmth that it was impossible not to feel relaxed as soon as you opened the door.

When I close my eyes and think of my grandmother, I see her standing in her kitchen by the stove, wearing her red apron, stirring a pot of something delicious. Smiling, she turns and opens her arms for me to run to her safe world of never-ending hugs, stories read in the old leather armchair, warm cinnamon buns and tales of olden days.

I have no memories of my grandmother rushing around. There was never anywhere else she needed to be other than right there with my sisters and I – time did not exist and she was always present. We played cards together when it was too rainy to go for walks. We read stories, we learnt to knit and then we baked and cooked. By the stove, we grew up, we laughed and we felt loved.

I don't think my grandmother ever consciously tried to set the scene for hygge moments; they were just always there and times with her were always hyggelige. If you ask me to describe a place where hygge is felt in abundance, it would be the space in which someone you love gives you all their time, asking for nothing in return but your company.

Our obsession with time is constant. We rush, every day, at speed, from place to place. To the bus, to our desks, to meetings, to the sandwich shop...We rush back home, we cook, we clean, we rush some more. Rush, rush, out again, doing all the things we have to do. Mustn't be late, like the rabbit in Alice in Wonderland. One of the rare times when most people usually stop rushing is when we go on vacation and when high seasons come around, like

Christmas day. At these special times we finally allow ourselves a bit of a break and this is often where we re-connect with the people we love. Inside these moments, on the beach in Marbella or curled up in front of the Sound of Music on Christmas day with a box of chocolates, this is hygge. Everybody looks forward to making these special moments – so why not ensure there is space for them on a Monday afternoon, too? What is stopping us?

No matter how much we dream of another few hours in the day, it won't ever happen. Instead, perhaps the answer lies in consciously carving out time to 'be' and reclaiming it, which is sort of what hygge asks you to do. We always find time to do the things we want to do, somehow. You find time to go to the hairdresser, you find time to go to the gym. If you make it important to, you can find time to sit down and just be, too – but only if you make it a priority.

Being present in the company of others is something we have become really, really bad at. Walk into any gathering of people and 90 per cent of them will be on their phones. This is often the case even at home. Mum and Dad – and sometimes children – on their phones and tablets, nobody talking and being present. We can't even wait for the bus for three minutes without staring at our screens. There is no doubt that

this is very damaging to everybody involved: we're missing all the fun. And if nobody in the space you are occupying is actually present, there is no hope of ever finding calm and relaxation – and definitely no hygge.

If we don't slow down and create pockets of time to be present, we are in danger of missing the moment entirely. We owe it to ourselves to take a break from chasing time because it keeps ticking, day in, day out – until, inevitably, we will realise it has run out.

Time is the most precious gift someone can give you. Inside the time they give, you will easily find hygge – because in this pocket of life are some of the tools we need to feel happy inside. Just sit down and take the time to feel it – and you will likely be rewarded. Grandparents, quite often, can be really good at doing this – maybe we can reconnect with them and re-learn the pleasures of not thinking we need to be somewhere else all the time.

SUPER-EASY CHOCOLATE OAT TREATS

Chokladbullar

All children in Scandinavia know how to make these. Simply the easiest no-bake treat to make – and utterly delicious to snack on. If you prefer less coffee flavour, you can leave it out and add a dash of milk or chocolate milk instead.

250 g/2¼ sticks butter

400 g/4 cups rolled oats

175 g/¾ cup caster/granulated sugar

4 tablespoons cocoa powder

4 tablespoons strong, cooled coffee

1 teaspoon vanilla sugar

desiccated/dried shredded coconut, sugar sprinkles or pearl sugar, to decorate

MAKES APPROX. 40

Blitz all the ingredients, except the coconut, sugar sprinkles or pearl sugar in a food processor or mix by hand (but allow the butter to soften before doing so).

Put the mixture in the fridge to firm up a bit before using or it can be a bit too sticky. Add more oats if you feel the mixture is too soft.

Roll into 2.5-cm/1-in. diameter balls, then roll each ball in either desiccated/dried shredded coconut, sugar sprinkles or pearl sugar.

Firm up in the fridge before eating – they will keep for up to a week in the fridge.

CHOCOLATE BISCUIT SLICES
Chokladsnittar

100 g/1 stick minus
1 tablespoon butter

80 g/¹/₃ cup caster/
granulated sugar

2 teaspoons vanilla sugar

1 teaspoon golden syrup/
light corn syrup

150 g/1 cup plain/
all-purpose flour

4 teaspoons cacao or cocoa
powder

1 teaspoon baking powder

pearl sugar or chopped
almonds, to decorate

*2 baking sheets, greased and
lined with baking parchment*

MAKES APPROX. 24

**These moreish biscuits/cookies are easy to make and
bake in super-quick time – the perfect accompaniment
to a cup of coffee.**

Preheat the oven to 180°C (350°F) Gas 4.

In a bowl, cream together the butter, caster/granulated
sugar and vanilla sugar. Add the syrup and mix well. In a
separate bowl, sift the dry ingredients together, then mix
into the wet mixture. Bring the mixture together with your
hands to form an even dough – it should not be sticky.

Split the dough into two lumps. Roll out each lump into a
6 x 35 cm/2¹/₂ x 14 in. rectangle, directly on the prepared
baking sheets.

Sprinkle the pearl sugar or chopped almonds down the
middle of the dough, then bake in the preheated oven for
about 10 minutes until almost baked through. As soon as
you remove them from the oven, use a pizza wheel or
sharp knife to cut each piece into 12 even-sized strips.

Leave to cool on a wire rack and store in an airtight
container for up to a week.

Note: See overleaf for the toffee biscuit slices.

140 g/1¼ sticks butter

120 g/½ cup caster/
granulated sugar

4 tablespoons golden syrup/
light corn syrup

1½ teaspoons vanilla sugar

1 teaspoon baking powder

300 g/2¼ cups plain/
all-purpose flour

½ teaspoon sea salt
(I use Malden), optional

*3 baking sheets, greased and
lined with baking parchment*

MAKES APPROX. 36

TOFFEE BISCUIT SLICES
Kolakakor

**A Swedish classic, these toffee biscuits/cookies are
super-quick to make. We like adding flakes of sea
salt to the top, but you can easily leave this out, if
you wish. (See photo on page 98.)**

Preheat the oven to 180°C (350°F) Gas 4.

In a bowl, cream the butter and caster/granulated sugar
until pale and fluffy, then add the syrup, followed by the
vanilla sugar, baking powder and flour. Mix with your hands
until you have an even dough.

Cut the dough into 3 equal pieces. Roll out to the size of
6 x 35 cm/2½ x 14 in. directly on the prepared baking
sheets. Sprinkle the salt over the top of the dough, if using.

Bake in the preheated oven for 8–10 minutes. As soon as
you remove the biscuits/cookies from oven, use a pizza
wheel or sharp knife to cut each rectangle into 12 pieces.

Leave to cool on a wire rack and store in an airtight
container for up to a week.

How to bring hygge into your life

Let go of time

Hygge is not dependent on time. You can't force it (or will it to happen) – you can't create a set time for it. Just let go of whatever it is you have planned later. If it happens, it happens. There is no time limit for hygge.

Let go of the phone

Being connected to the rest of the world is not necessary, because the only people you need to connect with are the ones in your company. Switch it off.

Eat nice stuff

The feeling of eating something yummy increases the comfort factor and our feelings of happiness. Hygge can absolutely happen without it – but to maximize the feeling, add a bowl of crisps/chips or sweets/candies to the table, or bake a nice cake. Cinnamon buns and hot chocolate work especially well here! Salads less so, but each to their own.

Be together

Share the space you are in – sit around the dinner table and keep talking, cosy up on the sofa with your mugs of hot chocolate and chat. Watch a movie together, one that makes you feel happy. Talk over it, because it's not about the movie really. Bake cupcakes with your kids and have a frosting fight in the kitchen. Whatever you do, be in a place where you are together and feel comfortable. Be the memory creator.

Don't try to make it happen

No amount of physical stuff can force the feeling of hygge. It's just stuff. Hygge happens in places where there is calm, love, time and space. It doesn't care if you live in a messy city studio – or if your house is minimalist designer. It doesn't care if you are rich or poor. Hygge is a feeling of appreciating your lot, in that time, in that space. Hygge is connecting with yourself and people around you. If you need candles to do that, then that's fine. If all you need is a cup of tea, a hug and a good old chat, that is absolutely perfect, too: It's inside you.

chapter 8

HYGGE AND... STRESS

Nobody lies on their deathbed wishing they'd worked harder and longer hours.

UNKNOWN

Some people thrive under a bit of pressure.

When deadlines loom, they suddenly spring into action and get everything done. When the pressure builds and builds, things start to crack. I know this because I frequently burn the candle at both ends, with to-do lists that are long and ambitious. Perhaps it is even slightly ironic that I am writing about stress and hygge – although hygge is where I find my personal sanctuary.

I can categorically confirm from experience that there are no hyggelige times to be found inside a stress bubble – for yourself or for the people around you. Stress is utterly devoid of any hyggelige feelings, no matter how many woolly blankets you try to wrap it in.

Over the past year, I have talked to many people about hygge and how to find space for hyggelige times in everyday life. The most frequent thing they say is that they don't have time to relax – by this, they mostly mean that they can't. When they finally sit down, their mind is still buzzing with activity, the phone is beeping with vital texts, there are Facebook posts to be written and tweets to check. Work doesn't stop when you leave your desk – the emails keep pinging. It's an instant reply world where you are on call 24/7 and there is no time to switch off because you might miss something really important, so you end up missing the moment you're in all together, for a moment in cyberspace.

When we feel stress in our bodies and stew on issues for a long time, our bodies produce cortisol. This gets us all fired up and we feel our engines running on all cylinders. Cortisol is a natural response in our bodies – we need it. It is part of the fight-or-flight mechanism that keeps us alert. When levels spike, the body is ready for action, ready to physically fight. In order to reduce cortisol, you need to have a release. But if you don't have a release, the levels just sit there in your body, causing all sorts of other issues.

If our cortisol levels spike for a prolonged period of time, it can interfere with our learning, memory, immune functions, blood pressure, and cholesterol, and can even make it harder to control our weight. If you have chronic levels of cortisol, you could also increase the risk of depression.

We don't tend to get release by sitting in front of a computer, so we need to find ways to diffuse this time bomb inside our bodies – or we potentially develop stress-related illness.

If we keep stress levels constantly high, eventually we might run the risk of having to deal with mental stress. However, while we're busy getting there (sometimes this is built up over years of bad habits), it's the people around us who are affected. We ourselves may not feel it, but our loved ones usually suffer even more than we do, because we're so busy being stressed that we have no time to feel anything.

It isn't as simple as just saying: 'I'm not going to be stressed anymore' and then following through. However, there are ways to slow things down a little and really make a difference – and allow yourself a bit of a break.

I'm not ashamed to say that I have been in a place of stress, and statistics say I am most certainly not alone. The thing that got me out of it in the end was the people I had been neglecting all along: my family and friends. I asked them what to do and they guided me back, quite simply, because none of the answers were complicated and mostly involved being present with them. I left my phone in another room, turned the ringer off and started breathing again. Slowly but surely, I found my old self by taking time out and making space for being together with 'my people'.

Effective ways to de-stress

Do something physical – be active. Get out there, do kick boxing, go for a walk or a run or play some football. Even if it is just walking the last two bus stops to work. Thirty minutes' movement a day is optimal. Get your body to release stress the natural way by using it. It's all wound up inside – moving it will unwind it, naturally.

Go to bed an hour earlier at night (sleep is a great healer). Mediate for 15 minutes a day when you wake up. If you don't have time to meditate daily for 15 minutes, you should meditate for an hour. If you don't like mediating at home, do some yoga, it provides part of what you need and it is also a good way to be physical.

Leave work on time. If leaving at 5.30pm is too much in the beginning, just try 30 minutes earlier, then move it to an hour earlier every day over time. Be strict with yourself on this: You didn't sell your soul to get a wage (anyway, you will be more effective if you know you have a set leaving time).

Switch off electronic devices. Allow yourself to disconnect from the world, even if it's just for a few hours a day. Buy an alarm clock that isn't your phone – leave your phone in a different room to the one you sleep in.

Be together with other people, be more social, surround yourself with love and make sure you also have proper downtime with yourself. This is where hygge comes in. In order to consciously create pockets of time where hygge may be found, you have to first remove all time restrictions and annoying electronic devices and just settle in to the moment. Even if it's hard in the beginning, it becomes easier over time.

DANISH VANILLA COOKIES
Vaniljekranse

1 whole vanilla pod/bean

250 g /1¹/₄ cups caster/granulated sugar

250 g/2¹/₄ sticks cold butter, cubed

325 g/scant 2¹/₂ cups plain/all-purpose flour

a pinch of salt

1 teaspoon baking powder

75 g/²/₃ cup ground almonds

1 egg

50 g/¹/₄ cup finely chopped almonds

3–4 baking sheets, greased and lined with baking parchment

a strong, fabric piping/pastry bag fitted with a large star nozzle/tip

MAKES 40

Around the world, people buy Danish butter cookies in pretty tins, but they taste nothing like the home-made version. While writing this book, I had many discussions with friends about how to recreate a recipe that tasted 'just like Grandma's', and found that it was harder than I first thought. Truth be told, nothing can replace the taste of those cookies that she made – there was so much love in them, heaven and earth together can't find a substitution. Still, after much trying, these do taste almost like my *Mormor* Erna's did. I hope that one day, my grandkids will bake these and say they taste just like Grandma Brontë's.

Grind the whole vanilla pod/bean, including the skin, with 3 tablespoons of the caster/granulated sugar in a spice grinder or food processor. Sift out any big lumps and set aside.

In a stand mixer or food processor, combine the cold butter with the plain/all-purpose flour, a pinch of salt, baking powder and the vanilla sugar mixture. Mix with the paddle attachment or pulse briefly, until the mixture has a coarse, sandy texture.

continued over page

continued from previous page

Add the ground almonds and remaining caster/granulated sugar and mix again, then add the egg and chopped almonds. Mix until you have an even dough that is soft enough to push through a piping/pastry bag. Note: you will need a strong fabric piping bag for this and a larger nozzle as the dough is really, really hard to push out. It may help to warm the dough with your hands until mouldable. Alternatively, you can also simply roll these, but they will not have the pattern.

Pipe (or roll) the dough into 8-10 cm/3¼-4 in. long sausages. Carefully connect the two ends of each to form rings and place on the prepared baking sheets. Make sure the dough is no thicker than the width of your little finger, because these will spread during baking.

Chill the dough rings on the baking sheets in the refrigerator for at least 30 minutes. This will help the cookies to keep their piped pattern as they bake.

Preheat the oven to 200°C (400°F) Gas 6.

Pop the cold baking sheets into the preheated oven and bake the cookies for 8-10 minutes, or until the edges are just slightly tinged golden brown. Remove from the oven and allow to cool and harden before eating. Store in an airtight container as the biscuits do go soft quickly.

180 g/1 cup caster/
granulated sugar

2 eggs

1 generous tablespoon plain/
all-purpose flour

1 teaspoon baking powder

100 g/1 cup rolled oats

20 g/1¹/₂ tablespoons rye
flakes (or plain rolled oats)

a pinch of salt

a drop of vanilla extract

50 g/3¹/₂ tablespoons
butter, melted

50 g/2 oz. dark/bittersweet
chocolate, melted

*2 baking sheets, greased and
lined with baking parchment*

MAKES APPROX. 30

NORDIC OAT CRISP BISCUITS

Havrekakor

A simple, quick, tasty treat and one of the more traditional Swedish fika bakes.

In a bowl, whisk the sugar and eggs until fluffy. In a separate bowl, sift together the flour and baking powder, then mix into the sugar and egg mixture with the oats, rye flakes (or extra oats), salt and vanilla. Stir together well. Pour in the melted butter, stirring until well combined. Leave for 15 minutes before using.

Preheat the oven to 200°C (400°F) Gas 6.

Drop tablespoons of the mixture onto the prepared baking sheets, leaving at least 5 cm/2 in. between the biscuits as they will spread out a lot during baking.

Bake in the preheated oven for 5 minutes – the biscuits are done once they have a slight brown colour. Remove from oven, then transfer with a spatula to a cold surface to cool.

Decorate the biscuits with drizzles of melted chocolate. Leave to dry, then store in an airtight container.

DAIM COOKIES

Daimkakor

150 g/1¼ sticks butter

300 g/2 cups plus 2 tablespoons plain/all-purpose flour

½ teaspoon bicarbonate of/baking soda

½ teaspoon vanilla sugar OR extract OR the seeds from 1 vanilla pod/bean

¼ teaspoon sea salt

150 g/¾ cup light brown soft sugar

100 g/½ cup caster/granulated sugar

1 egg

1 egg yolk

2 tablespoons whole milk

5 Daim bars (each weighing 28 g/1 oz.), roughly chopped

2 baking sheets, greased and lined with baking parchment

MAKES 20-22 COOKIES (DEPENDING ON HOW MUCH DOUGH YOU EAT!)

These cookies are wonderfully gooey and filled with pieces of delicious chocolate-coated almond toffee. Daim is one of the most popular chocolate bars in Sweden. You can use another type of chocolate bar if you can't get hold of Daim.

Melt the butter and set aside to cool down.

Combine flour, bicarbonate of/baking soda, vanilla and salt in a bowl and set side.

Combine the sugars with the cooled, melted butter and stir until no lumps remain. Combine the egg, egg yolk and milk and mix with the sugar and butter until thoroughly combined.

Add the flour, bit by bit, mixing until everything is incorporated. Add the Daim pieces and mix to combine. Wrap the dough in clingfilm/plastic wrap and place in the refrigerator to chill for a few hours.

Preheat the oven to 190°C (375°F) Gas 5.

Form the dough into rough balls, each weighing about 40 g/1½ oz. and place on the prepared baking sheets around 5 cm/2 in. apart.

Bake in the preheated oven for 8-10 minutes or until just golden. Remove from the oven immediately and transfer to a cooling rack – the middle should still be slightly soft but they will harden up after a while. The cookies will be at their very best about half an hour after removing from the oven.

chapter 9

HYGGE AND... SOUL

*Ordinary riches can be stolen;
real riches cannot. In your soul
are infinitely precious things
that cannot be taken from you.*

OSCAR WILDE

It is hard to know where hygge as a cultural concept ends and where it begins as something that can be translated and transferred into another language.

Hygge has been part of the Nordic countries for so long and, in its current form, hailed as the great beacon of Danish culture. How do you translate it into another language without losing the little nuances that makes hygge what it is to every Dane, Norwegian and Swede you meet along the way?

I wasn't surprised when the hygge backlash began. For such a gentle, unassuming concept, being thrust into the limelight was not unlike someone winning a TV talent show and having to deal with fame overnight. Almost anyone or anything that gets thrust into the spotlight will be misunderstood at times – and quite possibly dropped from a great height as quickly as it arrived.

It's a shame to regard hygge as a one-hit wonder, because if you really take time to understand it – and embrace it – it can have an immense effect on your soul and the way you consciously choose to live your life. You may decide to not call it hygge – but the point is the same: remembering to appreciate the moment you're in, when you're in it.

While we have to conform, to some extent, to the society in which we choose to live, our soul is always our own. It requires us to feed it, to nurture it and to keep it alive at all times. While we all know this, the first thing we neglect when we rush around too much is our own heart, our own needs and desires. It's easy to kid ourselves that we can find solace and happiness in our day jobs (few people can). Can we ever truly meet our potential unless we allow space for things to just happen and for life to take us in different directions?

In hygge, there is the breathing space that so many people forget about. There is relaxation and there is soul nourishment. That hygge is often a social event means you naturally spend the time with people you actually like and want to be together with – and less with people you don't (that's okay, you know).

Is hygge going to make you happy? Maybe not. Will it make you popular and will setting aside time for it mean you'll never be sad again? Nope. Hygge is not your saviour. Hygge didn't develop in order to be made into a self-help phenomenon. Never in its existence did hygge ever claim to do all of those things that so many books and magazines and articles now hail it for. Hygge is the little things you do alongside the mindfulness, the breathing, the yoga, the sport, the therapy – the thing that calmly sits alongside and allows you to appreciate the journey.

On the flipside, hygge has been embraced by the whole world just when we needed it most – that thing, that little thing we forget to do that is so simple and easy to reintroduce: togetherness. Being present with your own soul and other souls in the same moment and time – sharing in this appreciation that you have the opportunity to actually do that. Letting go of the day's stress, allowing your soul to be in the driving seat for a little while. Now, THAT is hygge. You can't label it, you can't say it's the same as cosiness or say that other words mean the same because hygge is an emotion that simply exists in order for people to remind themselves that all they need to do right now, at that exact moment in time, is be. Just be.

To some, it's down the pub with friends. To others, it's in a spa. To my Mum, it's playing cards and drinking a cup of coffee on the terrace. To me, it's baking with my kids and making cookies or taking a walk with my wonderful father. It's in finding my Christmas spirit, it's in a tent and it's sometimes at work. The one thing hygge is not, is labelled. Everybody's soul needs feeding at times. We need to remember to reignite the stuff that makes us appreciate our lives, our situations – even if we have to look closely at the little things and add them all up.

RUM TREATS

Romkugler

500 g/1lb. leftover Danish pastries and/or cake – ideally a mixture of both

2–3 tablespoons good quality raspberry jam/jelly

100 g/³/₄ cup icing/confectioners' sugar (add less if your cakes are a really sweet variety)

100 g/7 tablespoons softened butter

2 tablespoons cocoa powder

vanilla extract

2–3 teaspoons rum extract or essence (I use quite a concentrated one – you may need to add a bit more, as you want it to have a good punchy flavour)

a handful of oats (optional)

dark or light chocolate vermicelli strands, to finish

MAKES 10–15

A true 'waste not, want not' treat. Every Danish bakery has loads of cakes that are, like these *romkugler* or rum balls, basically made from leftover pastries. It makes a lot of sense for bakers to find ways to use their leftovers in really delicious ways. I usually use a cinnamon swirl or two, some sponge cake and maybe some chocolate cake or a muffin.

Roughly tear any Danish pastries into bite-sized pieces and crumble up any cakes you are using. In a stand mixer using the paddle attachment or in a food processor, blend the shredded and crumbled pastries and cakes with the rest of the ingredients (apart from the oats and the chocolate vermicelli) until evenly mixed. Alternatively, you can do this by hand with a wooden spoon in a mixing bowl, but it will take longer.

Taste the mixture – it may need more cocoa powder, rum extract or even icing/confectioners' sugar. Because this is made with leftovers, the taste will vary a bit. If you feel it needs more texture, you can add a handful of oats.

Chill the mixture in the refrigerator for about an hour to firm up.

Roll into balls a bit larger than the size of a golf ball and roll in the chocolate vermicelli strands to evenly coat. Chill again in the refrigerator until you are ready to serve.

Rum treats will keep well for 2–3 days wrapped in clingfilm/plastic wrap and stored in the refrigerator.

CRISPY SWEET WAFFLES

Frasvåfflor

150 g/1¼ sticks butter, melted, plus a little extra for greasing

300 g/2¼ cups plain/all-purpose flour

2 teaspoons baking powder

1 teaspoon vanilla sugar OR extract OR use the seeds from 1 vanilla pod/bean

250 ml/1 cup plus 1 tablespoon whole milk

250 ml/1 cup plus 1 tablespoon water

cloudberry or strawberry jam/jelly and whipped cream, OR vanilla bean syrup and fresh fruit, to serve (optional)

a heart-shaped waffle iron – available online. You can use a different shaped iron, but cooking time and yield may vary

MAKES 16

You may think that a waffle is just a waffle – but there are different types. These ones are called *frasvåfflor* and are crispier, best eaten straight away. This recipe is from my mother-in-law, Eva. She makes these for us when we visit their house in Sälen in Sweden. After spending the precious daylight hours in the snow on the mountains where they live, we'll get back to the cottage and warm up in front of the log fire. Then we all gather at the table to eat freshly made *frasvåfflor*.

Heat up the waffle iron and brush with melted butter.

Mix all the ingredients (apart from the serving suggestions) together to form a smooth batter.

Add a ladle full of batter to the preheated waffle iron and close the lid. Leave to cook for 2–3 minutes or until golden brown and crispy. Remove and serve immediately with plenty of cloudberry or strawberry jam/jelly and whipped cream. Repeat with the remaining batter.

Vanilla bean syrup: To make a quick vanilla bean syrup to serve with the waffles, combine 150 g/¾ cup caster/granulated sugar with the seeds from 1 vanilla bean/pod and 100 ml/⅓ cup water. Bring to the boil, then simmer for 4–5 minutes over a high heat, taking care not to let the mixture bubble over or the sugar burn. If it's reducing too quickly, shorten the cooking time or you will end up with a syrup that's too thick. Remove from the heat and add sea-salt flakes to taste. Pour over the waffles to serve.

VÄSTERBOTTEN AND SPINACH WAFFLES

Västerbottensvåfflor
Med spenat

100 g/1 stick minus 1 tablespoon butter, melted, plus extra for greasing

150 g/1 cup plain/all-purpose flour

75 g/½ cup wholegrain spelt flour

2 teaspoons baking powder

75 g/¾ cup finely grated Västerbotten cheese (or mature/sharp Cheddar)

100 g/½ cup blanched, cooked spinach, or 3–4 frozen balls (defrosted), liquid squeezed out and chopped

a pinch of salt

freshly ground black pepper

150 g/1½ cups chopped, cooked smoked bacon pieces/pancetta

sour cream, to serve (optional)

a heart-shaped waffle iron – available online. You can use a different shaped iron, but cooking time and yield may vary

MAKES 7–8

On one of those days where only an abundance of cheese will do, you will find me hogging all the *Västerbotten* to myself – it's such a delicious Swedish cheese. I make these waffles on cold winter days when the rain and sleet forces us to cosy up inside. This is the perfect low-effort snack – just throw everything together and cook in the waffle iron. Jonas, my husband, loves the bacon/pancetta pieces in these waffles – but you can omit if preferred.

Heat up the waffle iron and brush with melted butter.

Combine all the ingredients (apart from the sour cream) together with 350 ml/1½ cups water and stir to incorporate and form a smooth, thick batter.

Add a ladle of batter to the hot waffle iron. Close the lid and cook for 2–3 minutes or until golden brown.

Remove from the pan and serve immediately with sour cream if liked.

chapter 10

HYGGE AND... NATURE

*Nature does not hurry yet
everything is accomplished.*

LAO TZU

We are outdoor people in Scandinavia.

We have a massive playground as our countries are spread over such a huge area – and with so few people (Norway, for example, has 15 people per square kilometre compared to the UK's 269). There are practically no people the further north you go, so there's plenty of space to run around in and find yourself. Our landscape spans far and wide – from the snow-topped fjells of Norway and the Arctic Circle – all the way down to flat Denmark, with no mountains at all.

It is no secret that being outside, getting some daylight and moving our bodies is good for us. It releases all the great chemicals in the brain and lifts the mood of even the gloomiest person. Breathing is central to all relaxation techniques – and where better to 'breathe' than in a place full of fresh air and life? Our souls are fed and we feel happier and more free.

Hygge is often portrayed as an indoor thing; something that happens under a blanket and only when there is a log fire nearby. This is not necessarily the case – because hygge is never dependent on a specific season, time of day or location.

Being outside and enjoying nature can absolutely be a part of what it means to hygge – nowhere more so than in Norway, probably the most outdoorsy of all of the Scandinavian countries. Norwegians are outside people and nature lovers all year round – especially when you give them a few fjells full of snow that they can ski down or a valley they can hike through. Outdoors is where Norwegians are happiest – the further away from the city, the better.

One of the easiest ways to bring hygge with you outside is to go for a nice long walk with friends. Just go for a stroll, with the walk being your only purpose – and maybe stop for a coffee and a bite to eat along your merry way. As always, the whole point of hygge is about being present in the moment and just letting go for a while. Admittedly, it is harder to hygge if you run a marathon – the actual strain of the run isn't very hyggeligt – so hyggelige outdoor activities tend to be centered around things that are calm and gentle

to do – and often things that can be enjoyed with other people. Walking the dog, going for a hike, spending time at the beach, going skiing or simply taking a picnic outside are all great ways to hygge.

The long summer days are perfect for enjoying an outdoor lifestyle. Camping is a great way to experience nature close up and to slow things down by cooking your food on an open fire in the evenings and waking up to the sound of the birds singing in the morning (incidentally, there is an actual word for this in Swedish – it is called 'Gökotta', which means 'a dawn picnic for purpose of going to hear the birds sing').

There is a certain freedom in not having a plan for the day and seeing where nature takes you – and there is also an amazing connection to be had to the planet we live on when we stop for a moment, take a deep breath and appreciate the beauty of Mother Nature. In the long summer days, I am always reminded of when I was a child and those days seemed to go on for ever and ever – just being outside and discovering plants, berries and secret hiding places and getting sun-kissed cheeks. As an adult, I try to recreate these memories with my own children. We picnic, we run, we skip and I try to climb a tree now and then (rather impractical for a 40-something woman with inappropriate shoes, but it is fun trying). Losing yourself in things that make you happy is the epitome of hygge itself – as long as you remember to stop and appreciate it as you do it, even for a split second.

Spending more time outside doesn't have to be an ominous task – simply adding a short walk to your daily routine (with or without dog/friend/family for company) is something that is so easy to start to do for most people – and a very effective way to start reclaiming a bit of personal time to just think and be.

APPLE AND CLOUDBERRY CRUMBLE

Smulpaj med äpple & hjortron

6 Granny Smith apples (or equivalent tart apples)

2 tablespoons freshly squeezed lemon juice

seeds from 1/2 vanilla pod/bean

200 g/2/3 cup cloudberry jam/preserve

vanilla ice cream or fresh vanilla custard, to serve

CRUMBLE TOPPING:

100 g/3/4 cup plain/all-purpose flour

80 g/3/4 cup ground almonds

40 g/1/4 cup chopped hazelnuts or almonds

100 g/7 tablespoons butter

100 g/1/2 cup golden caster/granulated sugar

a pinch of sea salt

flaked/slivered almonds (optional)

SERVES 4-6

The humble cloudberry is probably the most sought-after berry in the Nordic countries. Very difficult to cultivate, the berries mostly grow in the wild far north and have a short season lasting only a few weeks. Cloudberries grow on stalks and look a bit like raspberries, although orange in colour.

Preheat the oven to 180°C (350°F) Gas 4.

Peel and core the apples and cut into bite-sized pieces. Place in a saucepan with a dash of water. Heat and stir for a few minutes, then add the lemon juice and vanilla seeds. Turn off the heat and fold in the cloudberry jam/preserve (if you are lucky and you can get hold of fresh cloudberries, use half cloudberries and half cloudberry jam/preserve, but reduce the amount of lemon juice a bit as fresh cloudberries are very tart).

To make the crumble topping, blitz all the ingredients apart from the flaked/slivered almonds in a food processor, until you have a crumbly mixture.

Add the apples to an ovenproof dish and top evenly with the crumble mixture. Add flaked/slivered almonds, if using, to the top of the crumble for extra crunch.

Bake in the preheated oven for about 25–30 minutes or until cooked.

Serve with a good vanilla ice cream or vanilla custard.

250 g/2½ cups spelt flour

100 g/½ cup light brown soft sugar

75 g/1 cup rolled/old-fashioned porridge oats, plus extra for topping

½ teaspoon salt

1 teaspoon bicarbonate of/baking soda

2 teaspoons baking powder

1 teaspoon vanilla sugar OR extract OR use the seeds from 1 vanilla pod/bean

1½ teaspoons ground cinnamon

½ teaspoon grated nutmeg

2 eggs

200 ml/¾ cup whole milk

75 ml/⅓ cup sunflower oil

2 teaspoons apple sauce or compote

2 teaspoons maple syrup

2 ripe bananas

100 g/¾ cup frozen or fresh blueberries

a muffin tray/pan lined with large tulip muffin cases, or regular muffin cases

MAKES 6–7 LARGE OR 10–12 SMALL

BLUEBERRY STUDMUFFINS

Blåbärsmuffins

At the café, people were always asking for a breakfast option that wasn't too 'green' but also not overly sweet. Our wholesome studmuffins are somewhere between a healthy muffin and those sugary ones you find at many coffee shops.

Preheat the oven to 180°C (350°F) Gas 4.

Combine all the dry ingredients in a mixing bowl and stir them together.

Mix all the wet ingredients together in another large bowl (apart from the bananas and berries). Add the wet ingredients to the dry ingredients and mix using a wooden spoon until just combined.

Roughly mash the bananas and add to the mixture. If using frozen blueberries, fold these in now. Portion out the batter into the muffin cases. If using fresh blueberries, add these to the batter now. Top each muffin with a scattering of porridge oats.

Bake in the preheated oven for about 30 minutes or until a skewer inserted into the middle comes out clean. The baking time will vary depending on the size of the muffins. Cool on a wire rack.

chapter 11

HYGGE AND... STUFF

Collect moments,
not things.

UNKNOWN

One of the most puzzling moments in the hygge revolution was when I was asked how to de-clutter in order to hygge.

I really didn't understand the question at first, because associating hygge with tidying up isn't something I would usually do. To most Scandinavians, hygge is such an emotional state of being – and de-cluttering, at least to me, is one of the most physical and boring things I can possibly think of spending my time doing. It's up there with taking out the trash and cutting the grass. Satisfying, perhaps, even necessary at times, but I don't find it at all hyggeligt to do, nor helpful in order to feel hygge more often.

I thought about it for ages and wondered how hygge had become a thing about tidying up and keeping a minimalist and de-cluttered house. What was it that made people think they had to reorganize things in order to feel relaxed and in the moment? Was I perhaps doing it wrong and should I head out to buy garbage bags and get started? It didn't feel right, at least to me.

Eventually I concluded that it must be a personal thing. What is relaxing to one person isn't necessarily relaxing to the next (and to be fair, I do think my youngest sister actually de-clutters for fun at times, but that is a separate matter and one I absolutely don't get involved in).

Personally, while I don't love living in a complete state of chaos, I don't mind a bit of washing up in the sink and I don't ever feel I must vacuum before people pop over. If you come to my house, don't expect a place ready for a photo shoot – and do expect to step on a few Lego bricks (strategically placed by my kids in order to inflict maximum grown-up cries of pain, which is always fun). I don't think having a house that isn't perfect has impacted on my ability to create a space where people I love feel happy, relaxed and hyggelige.

One of the very best places to hygge is in a British pub. How can you not feel totally at ease and relaxed in a good old country inn with a pint of ale in your hand? Also, pubs are never short of being full of 'stuff', from pictures of the village football team's wins over the years to knick-knacks on every shelf – as far away from a stereotypical Scandinavian house as you can possibly get. There are no clean lines, no colour-coded bookshelves. I'd go as far to say a British pub is rather distant from what most people would consider minimalist living – here it is all about warmth – and warmth is where hygge starts for many people.

When you go to Scandinavia, you see that a lot of the places where we find hygge are not that far from the British idea of hygge down the pub, except we don't really go to pubs as such as it isn't part of our culture – but spaces in the same style also exist in Scandinavia. Take, for example, the Nordic cottage life. From your Norwegian mountain huts to your Swedish ski lodge to your Danish beach house…these are also not what most people outside Scandinavia perceive as 'typical Scandi design', but very much feature on the more rustic scale of interiors. We actually also love little knick-knacks, we love old things and, in general, we really don't mind a bit of clutter here and there. Just make sure there is an Arne Jacobsen chair somewhere nearby, or a really cool lamp, to make us feel safe. But getting rid of your 'stuff' solely in order to create hygge? Never.

Everyone is different. What makes you feel relaxed in your own space really is a personal thing and there are no amount of how-to lists and guidebooks that can help you get there. If your personal idea of happiness is clean lines, de-cluttered cupboards and a newly polished floor then by all means, go ahead and get it sorted. Or, just relax into that old armchair with the floral pattern, surrounded by your collection of teapots, if that's what does it for you: your hygge is entirely your own.

SEED CRISPBREAD
Fröknäcke

50 g/¼ cup sesame seeds

70 g/½ cup sunflower seeds

70 g/½ cup pumpkin seeds

50 g/½ cup flaxseeds/linseeds

20 g/1 tablespoon plus 1 teaspoon chia seeds

50 g/⅓ cup buckwheat flour

pinch of xanthan gum

50 ml/3½ tablespoons rapeseed/canola oil

150 ml/⅔ cup boiling water

pinch of sea salt, plus extra for sprinkling

2 large baking sheets, greased and lined with baking parchment

MAKES 2 LARGE SHEETS (ROUGHLY 20 SMALLER PIECES)

For those of us who stick to a no-gluten way of eating, having a recipe for a crispbread that isn't hard to make is really useful. This easy crispbread is full of seed goodness, too. My mother-in-law Eva kindly shared her recipe for this crispbread and we have since adapted it with extra seeds and buckwheat flour. If you don't worry about the gluten, you can use plain/all-purpose flour instead of the naturally gluten-free buckwheat flour (in this case, you can also omit the xanthan gum).

Preheat the oven to 150°C (300°F) Gas 2.

Combine all the ingredients in a bowl and stir. You will have a jelly-like consistency mixture, not a dough.

Place half the mixture on one sheet of baking parchment. Place another sheet of baking parchment on top and roll out as evenly and thinly as possible. Carefully remove the parchment. The mixture will remain sticky.

Repeat on the second baking sheet. Sprinkle a little extra salt to the top of each and place in the oven.

Bake for 50–60 minutes until it is crispy and completely baked through.

Remove from the oven and allow to cool slightly before breaking into large pieces. Store in an airtight container.

Hygge for sale

Throughout my whole life living in Scandinavia – and being a proud Dane – I honestly do not think I have ever seen hygge as a brand. No hygge blankets, socks, shoes, sweaters, curtains, underpants… nothing.

To us, selling an emotional state is frankly quite an odd thing. The word hygge has such value for us that branding almost devalues it – which is what has happened to some extent since hygge moved away from home and became an international superstar.

You wouldn't brand other emotions this way… Sadness socks? Happiness underpants? Consumerism wants us to buy, buy, buy, so to hell with the meaning: just buy more stuff.

You don't need to buy anything to feel hygge. All you need to do is slow down, relax and just appreciate the moment you are in, while you are in it. You don't need to mention it, talk about it, create it – just appreciate it.

Ingredients

200 g/7 oz. good-quality 70% dark/bittersweet chocolate

250 g/2¼ sticks unsalted butter

275 g/1½ cups minus 2 tablespoons caster/granulated sugar

3 eggs

75 g/½ cup plus 1 tablespoon plain/all-purpose flour

50 g/2 oz. good-quality cocoa powder (I use Fazer cacao)

a pinch of salt

1 teaspoon vanilla sugar OR extract OR use the seeds from 1 vanilla pod/bean

150 g/5 oz. filling of your choice – see end of method for suggestions

a 20 x 20-cm/8 x 8-in. square baking pan, greased and lined with baking parchment

MAKES 9–12

LOKI'S BROWNIE
Lokis chokoladekage

A good chocolate brownie rarely fails to satisfy. At the café, we have lots of different bits and pieces left over that work with chocolate, so our Kitchen Angels often make this easy brownie base and add whatever good stuff they feel like – from chocolate bars to sweets and fruit or nuts. The name, Loki, comes from Norse mythology. Loki was a trickster god and also a shape-shifter. This brownie often shape-shifts at the café: it may not be quite what it was the last time you had it, hence the name. Experiment with adding your own treats to the mix.

Preheat the oven to 170°C (340°F) Gas 4.

Melt the chocolate and butter in a heatproof bowl set over a pan of barely simmering water. Do not let the base of the bowl touch the water. Alternatively, you can melt the chocolate in the microwave, but take care to just melt, don't cook it. Set aside to cool.

Beat together the caster/granulated sugar and eggs by hand using a balloon whisk in a large mixing bowl. There is no need to beat in loads of air as you don't want the brownie to rise too much. Ensure the melted chocolate-butter has cooled sufficiently, then stir it into the sugar-egg mixture.

continued over page

continued from previous page

Sift the plain/all-purpose flour, cocoa powder and salt into the bowl. Add the vanilla and fold with a spatula until smooth. Take care not to overwork the mixture. Fold in 100 g/3½ oz. of your chosen filling. Pour the mixture into the prepared pan and sprinkle the remaining filling on top.

Bake in the preheated oven for 25–30 minutes or until a skewer inserted into the side comes out clean – the middle can still be gooey but it should not wobble when you shake the pan. Leave to cool, then cut into squares to serve.

Filling suggestions: 150 g/5 oz. nuts such as walnuts, pecans, macadamias or Brazil nuts. Your favourite sweets/candy: marshmallows, chopped Daim bars, toffees/caramels, liquorice, soft nougat praline chunks, mint chocolates or chocolate buttons. Dried fruit such as raisins or cherries.

Note: Baking times will vary. Brownies are quite forgiving if you cook them on lower heat for a longer time – so keep checking the edges and just make sure you don't overbake. It's better to slightly underbake a brownie, if anything, so take it out a bit earlier rather than give it that extra few minutes.

chapter 12

HYGGE AND... YOUR HOME

A house is not a home.

UNKNOWN

It is important to separate stereotypical Scandinavian interiors from what it is that makes something hyggeligt.

I talk a lot to people about how they don't need to buy new things in order to create a space for more hygge in their lives. It is only natural that people look to the Nordics as the birthplace of hygge for inspiration, and what people see is the way we tend to live, physically. The Scandinavian home and style have become synonymous with hygge, even though the physical items play little or no part in the feeling people seek. What people associate with Scandinavia is our nature, design, style and our way of life. Inside all of these things, you find pockets of hygge.

All countries have different styles, reflecting their culture and heritage. These have little bearing on how hyggelige a room may or may not end up being – it is more important that you fill the rooms with people and love. I think it can be a mistake to use the typical Scandinavian home to illustrate the ideal space for more hygge. The truth is, no amount of candle holders or vases will ever make a house into a home.

A home is what happens when you fill a space with things that make you feel safe. It is a sense of creating comfort behind closed doors. Our private space holds the key to our wellbeing and self-expression: it is the place where we live and where we love. The place where we feel so comfortable that we can do the vacuuming in our underpants and the place we create memories with the people closest to us. You're not going to be yourself in your own home unless that space reflects part of who you are – and you will not feel relaxed, either.

If what you aspire to and what makes you happy is a Scandinavian-style home, then go for it. Paint all the walls white and throw away all your bulky furniture. Have really neat shelves and fewer 'things'. Subscribe to the 'less is more' rule and buy stylish designer lamps. Do not, however, assume this will deliver hygge.

I constantly see beautiful photos of pretty rooms, people Instagramming nice crockery, smart notebooks and a pretty vase, captioned with 'Look at how hygge my table is'. Stylish shots of living rooms, fireplaces, blankets, a pair of slippers. It always makes me ask: But where are the people? Without life, there is no hygge – only the teasing premise that there could be hygge, once you fill the space with people. This is also, importantly, the moment where hygge becomes separated from the feeling of cosiness – because cosy is physical as well as emotional, whereas hygge is only ever emotional and is never bound by material things.

Hygge is most often a social event. It needs you to fill the room, because without people, it is just a physical space where only the potential of hygge can exist. Your soul is in the room, your time is there, your emotional energy is there. On your own, at peace with yourself, you find hygge and calm in your own space, and quite often this is in your own home. With others in this space, you share and create memories in the same space and you find hygge in appreciating the things you share there, as they happen around you.

There are, of course, physical things that increase and enhance your feeling and sharing of hygge in your space. A bowl of treats can help. A mug of something warm, sipped as you sit on your sofa, chatting to your best friend about old times. The notebook, so carefully laid out in the Instagram shot, may help you find hygge when you fill it with your thoughts and feelings or the opening paragraphs of that novel you have always wanted to write. A few candles lit for atmosphere and to encourage your words to flow. All these things help set a scene, a premise of hygge – but it is never forced. And do you know what? Sometimes it just doesn't happen, either, even if your new scented candle smells of a meadow in the summer and you ate an entire bar of chocolate!

Hygge no-nos

There is an unwritten set of rules about what you should and shouldn't talk about in hygge. Very rarely are the following subjects discussed:

- People's professions
- Salary
- Politics
- Current affairs
- Religion

Because hygge is all about being in the moment together, strong opinions may separate the moment and remove the hyggelige feeling. Avoid introducing anything controversial.

What makes your house a home is you. My house is a home because it is filled with laughter and love. It is filled with baking and the smell of vanilla. It is filled with my family, and the things that make me happy – the old armchair found in a flea market that the kids fight over as they settle down to watch movies on a rainy day. Often a few dishes in the kitchen sink. Way too many books. Sure, my house may look quite Scandinavian, but that is only because it reflects where I come from. An empty room will only ever give you a canvas and the potential of hygge. It will never deliver it to you unless you fill it with heartbeats.

Hygge...

- Creates intimacy
- Appreciates the simple, shuns the complicated
- Forces you to be present in the moment
- Makes you connect with yourself or people around you
- Releases good feelings in your brain and makes you feel good
- Makes you relax
- Allows you to be kind to yourself
- Removes the phone and other devices that try to connect you to other spaces
- Releases you from the constraints of time, if only for a short while
- Reminds you that you, in that moment, feel content and maybe even happy.

INDEX

ACKNOWLEDGEMENTS

Thank you Jonas, Jeg elsker dig. Thank you for being everything, always. Astrid and Elsa, you make life into a long happy dance and my feet can't stop moving.

David Jørgensen, for the words you correct, for the words you say – and most importantly, for the ones you hold back! Your patience and friendship is everything.

Mark Davies, the man who never fails to remind me that 'present' is the only valuable space in which to live. Thank you.

Also thank you to the lovely, inspiring people at Ryland, Peters & Small, my amazing agent Jane Maw and everyone in our great team at ScandiKitchen.

PICTURE CREDITS:
All photography by Peter Cassidy apart from:
2 ferrantraite/Getty Images
4 Debi Treloar's home available to hire for shoots www.debitreloar.com. Ph Debi Treloar
7 Image Source/Getty Images
10 Nassima Rothacker
14 Debi Treloar
15 James Gardiner
18 Caiaimage/Francis Pictures/Getty Images
21 Fredrik Skold/Getty Images
23 Nassima Rothacker
24 Pekic/Getty Images
32 Debi Treloar
35 brittak/Getty Images
37 James Gardiner
45 Debi Treloar
46 William Reavell
49-50 Steve Painter
51 William Reavell
55 The home of Yvonne Eijkenduijn of www.yvestown.com in Belgium. Ph Catherine Gratwicke
62 Foster House, the family home of Atlanta Bartlett and Dave Coote, available to hire for photography through www.beachstudios.co.uk. Ph Polly Wreford
65 Nassima Rothacker
67 Richard Jung
71 William Lingwood
75 Catherine Gratwicke
78 The home of Birgitte and Henrik Moller Kastrup in Denmark. Ph Rachel Whiting
81 odmeyer/Getty Images
82 Matthew Micah Wright/Getty Images
83 Kate Whitaker
90 The family home of the architects Jeanette & Rasmus Frisk of www.arkilab.dk. Ph Ben Robertson
93 Caiaimage/Sam Edwards/Getty Images
95 www.instagram.com/chloeuberkid. www.uberkid.net. Ph Ben Robertson
102 James Gardiner
105 ArtesiaWells/Getty Images
107 Debi Treloar
110 William Reavell
114 Jo Henderson
119 Debi Treloar
126 Erin Kunkel
129 Geir Pettersen/Getty Images
130 Martin Brigdale
136 The home of Ida Susanne Collier of sukkertoyforoyet.blogspot.no. Ph Catherine Gratwicke
139 Simon Brown
141 Dorthe Kvist garden and interior designer, stylist, TV host, blogger and author. Ph Katya de Grunwald
147 Kate Whitaker
148 The home and shop of Katarina von Wowern of www.minaideer.se. Ph Rachel Whiting
151 Dorthe Kvist garden and interior designer, stylist, TV host, blogger and author. Ph Katya de Grunwald
152 Debi Treloar
153 Foster House, the family home of Atlanta Bartlett and Dave Coote, available to hire for photography through www.beachstudios.co.uk. Ph Polly Wreford
156 The family home of Nina Tolstrup and Jack Mama of www.studiomama.com. Ph Debi Treloar
157 Styling assistance by Debbie Johnson of Powder Blue – Styling Props Locations www.powder-blue.co.uk. Ph Debi Treloar